Ella Fitzgerald

THE CHICK WEBB YEARS & BEYOND
RON FRITTS and KEN VAIL

The Scarecrow Press, Inc.
Lanham, Maryland, and Oxford
2003

SCARECROW PRESS, INC.

Published in the United States of America
by Scarecrow Press, Inc.
A wholly owned subsidiary of
The Rowman & Littlefield Publishing Group, Inc.
4501 Forbes Boulevard, Suite 200, Lanham, Maryland 20706
www.scarecrowpress.com

PO Box 317
Oxford
OX2 9RU, UK

British Library Cataloguing in Publication Information Available

Library of Congress Cataloging-in-Publication Data Available

0-8108-4881-3 (pbk.: alk. paper)

♾™ The paper used in this publication meets the minimum requirements of American National Standard for Information Sciences—Permanence of Paper for Printed Library Materials, ANSI/NISO Z39.48-1992.
Manufactured in the United States of America.

Acknowledgments
Our grateful thanks to:
Rolf Dahlgren for his generosity in sharing his photographs;
Down Beat and *Metronome* magazines;
Franz Hoffmann for his amazing series of books, *Jazz Advertised*;
Bob Inman for his invaluable Swing Era Scrapbooks;
Michel Macaire of the Ella Fitzgerald Music Appreciation Society;
David Nathan of the National Jazz Foundation Archive at Loughton;
Brian Peerless for sharing his collection of *Metronomes* and *Down Beats* and much more besides;
Tony Shoppee for sharing his *Down Beat* collection;
Sharon Moats, Rhonda Rynex, Joel Reiff, Bob Lazon, Chris Sheridan, Donna Halper and Bill Buchanan for their assistance and encouragement;
Grant Elliott, Bob Frost, Dave Green, Jim Greig, Scott Hamilton, Dan Morgenstern, Hank O'Neal, Ken Peplowski, Bruce Phillips, Norman Saks, Randy Sandke and David Smith for help and encouragement at crucial moments.

We have also been grateful for the writings of Sid Colin, Geoffrey Mark Fidelman, Jim Haskins, Bud Kliment, Tom Lord, Stuart Nicholson, Phil Schaap, Barry Ulanov.

Photographs from the collections of Rolf Dahlgren, Frank Driggs, Brian Foskett, Bob Inman, David Redfern (William Gottlieb), Duncan Schiedt, Peter Vacher and the authors

Preface

The Jazz Itineraries set out to provide a fascinating insight into the life and times of some of my favourite jazz musicians, in this case… Ella Fitzgerald. Using contemporary photographs, newspaper reports, advertisements and reviews, I have attempted to chronicle her life through the Chick Webb years to the early days of Jazz at the Philharmonic. I have tried to include all known club, concert, television, film and jam session appearances as well as her recordings, although this is not intended to be a discography.

I hope that you will find this book an informative accompaniment when listening to Ella's records or reading any of her biographies.

Ken Vail, Cambridge, March 2003

Wednesday 25 April 1917
Ella Jane Fitzgerald is born in Newport News, Virginia, to Tempie Williams and William Fitzgerald. Tempie and William are not married and by the time Ella is 3-years-old, he has left. Tempie takes up with a Portuguese immigrant, Joe Da Silva, and they move to Yonkers in New York.

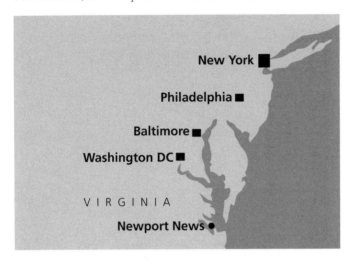

1923
Tempie gives birth to Frances, Ella's half-sister.

September 1923
Ella Fitzgerald (6) starts at Public School 10 in Yonkers. She also attends the Bethany African Methodist Episcopal Church where she develops a liking for singing.

September 1926
Ella Fitzgerald (9) begins fourth grade at Public School 18 in Yonkers. She is now a keen dancer.

September 1929
Ella Fitzgerald (12) enters Benjamin Franklin Junior High School in Yonkers.

early 1932
Ella's mother, Tempie Williams Fitzgerald (38), has a heart attack and dies.

21 April 1932
Aware of Joe Da Silva's treatment of his step-daughter, Tempie's sister Virginia takes Ella out of school and brings her home to W145th Street in Harlem.

1933
Ella is running wild in Harlem, missing school and flouting the law. She is caught and sent to the New York State Training School for Girls at Hudson, near Albany, New York.

1934
Ella runs away from the institution. Unable to go home, she lives on the streets in Harlem.

Wednesday 21 November 1934
Ella Fitzgerald enters the Amateur Night contest at the Apollo Theatre in Harlem. Backed by the Benny Carter Orchestra, she wins the contest.

1935

Friday 15 February 1935
Ella Fitzgerald makes her professional debut with Tiny Bradshaw's Band at the Harlem Opera House in New York.

Thursday 21 February 1935
Ella Fitzgerald and Tiny Bradshaw's Band close at the Harlem Opera House in New York City.

Friday 1 March 1935

Chick Webb and his Orchestra open a one-week engagement at the Harlem Opera House in New York.

During the week, vocalist Charles Linton brings 16-yr-old Ella to see Chick. Chick is unimpressed but he is persuaded to give Ella a trial during a two-week stint at the Savoy Ballroom immediately following the theatre engagement.

Thursday 7 March 1935

Chick Webb and his Orchestra close at the Harlem Opera House in New York City.

Friday 8 March 1935

Chick Webb and his Orchestra play a dance for the St. Elmo Fraternity at Yale University in New Haven, Connecticut. Ella is taken along for a try-out and is well-received by the white college crowd.

Saturday 9 March 1935

Chick Webb and his Orchestra open an engagement at the Savoy Ballroom in New York City. Ella's trial goes well and, despite her plain and awkward appearance, Chick is persuaded to take her on. Gradually, with help, Ella's appearance and dress sense improve. Webb's bookers, the Gale Agency, pay for a room for Ella at the Braddock Hotel on 126th Street and Eighth Avenue.

Left: 17-yr-old Ella with Charles Linton.

Thursday 21 March 1935

Ella and the Chick Webb Orchestra broadcast over WJZ from Radio City. This is the first in a regular afternoon series, every Thursday, Friday and Saturday.

Sunday 31 March 1935

Chick Webb and his Orchestra accompany Lily Pons, Helen Jepson and Gladys Swarthout at the Annual Operatic Surprise Party at the Metropolitan Opera House in New York City. Ella Fitzgerald does not appear.

Thursday 24 April 1935

Chick Webb and his Orchestra play a Benefit for Unemployed Musicians at the Savoy Ballroom in New York City. They play a Battle of the Bands versus the Casa Loma Orchestra.

Friday 25 April 1935

Ella's 17th birthday.

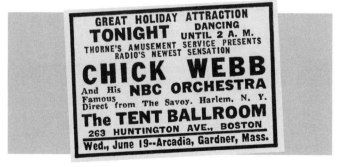

Saturday 4 May 1935

Ella Fitzgerald and the Chick Webb Orchestra play a dance at the Brooklyn Palace in New York City.

Wednesday 12 June 1935

Ella Fitzgerald (17) makes her first recording with the Chick Webb Orchestra for Decca in New York City.
ELLA FITZGERALD (vocal), MARIO BAUZA, TAFT JORDAN, REUNALD JONES (trumpets), SANDY WILLIAMS (trombones), EDGAR SAMPSON (alto sax), PETE CLARK (alto sax), ELMER WILLIAMS (tenor sax), DON KIRKPATRICK (piano), JOHN TRUEHEART (guitar), JOHN KIRBY (bass), CHICK WEBB (drums)
I'll Chase The Blues Away (vEF) / *Love And Kisses* (vEF)
The band also record an instrumental and a Charles Linton vocal: *Down Home Rag* / *Are You Here To Stay* (vCL)

Saturday 15 June 1935

Ella Fitzgerald and the Chick Webb Orchestra make the last of their afternoon broadcasts from Radio City as they prepare to go out on tour. The Teddy Hill Orchestra replaces them

Monday 17 June 1935

Ella Fitzgerald and the Chick Webb Orchestra play a dance at the Tent Ballroom in Boston.

Wednesday 19 June 1935
Ella Fitzgerald and the Chick Webb Orchestra play a dance at the Arcadia Dance Hall in Gardner, Massachusetts.

Tuesday 25 June 1935
Ella Fitzgerald and the Chick Webb Orchestra play a dance at the Savoy Ballroom in New York City. Also billed to appear are Willie Bryant, Teddy Hill, Fletcher Henderson, the San Domingans and the Fran Waring Orchestras. The honored guest, following his heavyweight fight with Primo Carnera, is Joe Louis.

Saturday 29 June 1935
Ella Fitzgerald and the Chick Webb Orchestra play a dance at the Hershey Park Ballroom in Hershey, Pennsylvania.

CHICK WEBB AND BAND NOW TOURING PENNA.

Chick Webb and his orchestra left Harlem Saturday morning en route to Harrisburg, Pa., where they will play an engagement and from there will tour the Keystone State for the week. The Chick will come by Washington on his way home.

Just back from Boston and a swing around the circle in New England, the famous "midget" maestro was flushed with the success of his second "Down East" tour.

Chick's records, made a few weeks ago for Decca, are proving popular hits with the public.

Monday 15 July 1935
Ella Fitzgerald and the Chick Webb Orchestra play a one-nighter at the Walker Ballroom in Indianapolis, Indiana.

Friday 19 July 1935
Ella Fitzgerald and the Chick Webb Orchestra open a one-week engagement at the Apollo Theatre in New York City.

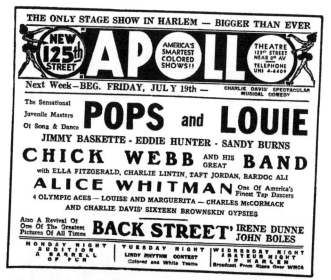

Thursday 25 July 1935
Ella Fitzgerald and the Chick Webb Orchestra close at the Apollo Theatre in New York City.

Sunday 28 July 1935
Ella Fitzgerald and the Chick Webb Orchestra play a Battle of the Bands versus the Julie Wintz Palisades Band at the Palisades Amusement Park in Fort Lee, New Jersey.

Chick Webb To Thrill At Club Mirador Aug.23

A big New York "name band" and the magic atmosphere of Western Pennsylvania's most beautiful night club!.

These two rare combinations, bringing the famous Chick Webb and his N.B.C. orchestra into the softly-lighted Club Mirador on Friday night, August 23, promises to draw one of the largest crowds of the season to the popular Homestead after-yawning rendezvous.

The popular Chick and his musically-talented Chicks, which created a sensation during their long and successful stay in the cosmopolitan Savoy Ballroom in New York City, is one of the most popular orchestras in the country and one of the favorite broadcasting bands. His return here is anxiously awaited by local dance lovers.

With its smooth, highly-polished dancing floor and its spacious seating accommodation for hundreds, the Club Mirador promises to be the perfect spot for such a big nationally-famous attraction like Chick Webb.

Friday 23 August 1935
Ella Fitzgerald and the Chick Webb Orchestra play a dance at the Club Mirador in Homestead, Pennsylvania.

Sunday 1 September 1935
Ella Fitzgerald and the Chick Webb Orchestra play a dance at the State Ballroom in Boston, Massachusetts.

Friday 13 September 1935
Ella Fitzgerald and the Chick Webb Orchestra play a dance at the Club Mirador in Homestead, Pennsylvania.

Saturday 12 October 1935
Ella Fitzgerald records with the Chick Webb Orchestra for Decca in New York City.
ELLA FITZGERALD (vocal), MARIO BAUZA, TAFT JORDAN, REUNALD JONES (trumpets), SANDY WILLIAMS (trombones), EDGAR SAMPSON (alto sax), PETE CLARK (alto sax), ELMER WILLIAMS (tenor sax), DON KIRKPATRICK (piano), JOHN TRUEHEART (guitar), BILL THOMAS (bass), CHICK WEBB (drums)
Rhythm And Romance (vEF) / *I'll Chase The Blues Away* (vEF)
The band also record an instrumental and vocals by Charles Linton and Taft Jordan: *Moonlight And Magnolias* (vCL) / *I May Be Wrong But I Think You're Wonderful* (vTJ) / *Facts And Figures*

Monday 14 October 1935
Ella Fitzgerald and the Chick Webb Orchestra play a Battle of the Bands versus Buddy Johnson at the Strand Theatre in Baltimore, Maryland.

Thursday 17 October 1935
Ella Fitzgerald and the Chick Webb Orchestra play a dance (9pm until 2am) at the Roseland Ballroom in Newport News, Virginia.

Sunday 27 October 1935
Ella Fitzgerald and the Chick Webb Orchestra play a Battle of the Bands versus Ruth Ellington Orchestra at the Cotton Club in Nashville, Tennessee.

Sunday 3 November 1935
Ella Fitzgerald and the Chick Webb Orchestra play a Battle of the Bands versus Jimmie Noone's Orchestra at the Savoy Ballroom in Chicago.

Tuesday 5 November 1935
Ella Fitzgerald and the Chick Webb Orchestra play a dance at the Pythian Temple Ballroom in Pittsburgh, Pennsylvania.

Friday 8 November 1935
Ella Fitzgerald and the Chick Webb Orchestra open a one-week engagement at the Apollo Theatre in New York City. Also on the bill are the Four Ink Spots, Sandy Burns, Jelli Smith, George Wiltshire, Apus Brooks, Jackie 'Moms' Mabley, Al Moore, the 3 Ragamuffins and Leonard Harper's Beauty Chorus.

CHICK WEBB 'World's Premier Drummer Brings His National Broadcasting Band to the Roseland Ballroom, Newport News, Virginia, Thursday Night, October 17th, 1935. FIVE HOURS OF DANCING NINE TO TWO ADMISSION 75c

First Appearance in Chicago
Chick Webb And His National Broadcasting Company ORCHESTRA Direct from New York City PLAYING AGAINST Jimmie Noone Sunday, Nov. 3rd Dancing 8:30 Until 2:00
30c Admission 30c Before 8:30 p.m. 40c—AFTER 8:30—40c
SAVOY BALLROOM 47th & SOUTH PARKWAY

APOLLO
4 INK SPOTS
CHICK WEBB AND HIS BAND
"Special Agent"
DON REDMAN

Thursday 14 November 1935

Ella Fitzgerald and the Chick Webb Orchestra close at the Apollo Theatre in New York City.

Friday 15 November 1935

Ella Fitzgerald and the Chick Webb Orchestra open a one-week engagement at Fays Theatre in Philadelphia. Also on the bill are the Four Ink Spots.

Thursday 21 November 1935

Ella Fitzgerald and the Chick Webb Orchestra close at Fays Theatre in Philadelphia.

Friday 22 November 1935

Ella Fitzgerald and the Chick Webb Orchestra open a one-week engagement at the Howard Theatre in Washington, D.C. Also on the bill are the Four Ink Spots, Brookes & Burns, Jelli Smith, George Wiltshire, and the 3 Cyclones.

Thursday 28 November 1935

Ella Fitzgerald and the Chick Webb Orchestra close at the Howard Theatre in Washington, D.C.

Monday 23 December 1935

Ella Fitzgerald and the Chick Webb Orchestra play a midnight dance (12.05am until 5.00am) at the New Albert Casino in Baltimore, Maryland.

1936

Ella Fitzgerald and the Chick Webb Orchestra return to their residency at the Savoy Ballroom in New York.

Chick Webb will air for NBC as a sustaining program from 9:30 to 10:00pm Fridays known as "The Harlem Hour."

Wednesday 22 January 1936

Ella Fitzgerald and the Chick Webb Orchestra are featured in a new WJZ radio programme, 'Gems of Color' from Radio City in New York. The weekly half-hour programme (9:30 to 10:00pm) also features the Four Ink Spots, Hamtree Harrington and the Cecil Mack Choir.

Wednesday 19 February 1936

Ella Fitzgerald and the Chick Webb Orchestra record radio transcriptions at the World Broadcasting Systems Studio at 711 Fifth Avenue in New York City.
ELLA FITZGERALD (vocal), MARIO BAUZA, TAFT JORDAN, BOBBY STARK (trumpets), SANDY WILLIAMS, CLAUDE JONES (trombones), EDGAR SAMPSON (alto sax), PETE CLARK (alto sax), ELMER WILLIAMS (tenor sax), WAYMAN CARVER (tenor sax/flute), DON KIRKPATRICK (piano), JOHN TRUEHEART (guitar), BILL THOMAS (bass), CHICK WEBB (drums)
Shine (vEF) / *Darktown Strutters Ball* (vEF) / *You Hit The Spot* (vEF) / *Rhythm And Romance* (vEF)

Friday 21 February 1936

Ella Fitzgerald and the Chick Webb Orchestra play opposite Fess Williams' Orchestra at the Savoy Ballroom in New York City.

Saturday 22 February 1936

Ella Fitzgerald and the Chick Webb Orchestra play a Scottsboro Defense Ball at the Savoy Ballroom in New York City.

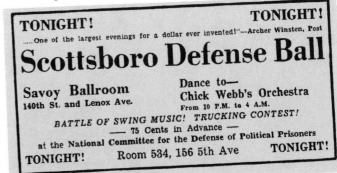

Sunday 23 February 1936

Chick Webb takes part in a UHCA jam session at the Famous Door in New York City. Also involved are Bunny Berigan, Bud Freeman and Dave Tough.

26 February—"Gems of Color" program was held up for revamping but will go on the air as soon as possible, headlining Chick Webb Orchestra

The revamped "Gems of Color" hit the ether waves with plenty of splash. Chick Webb, with Ella Fitzgerald on vocal, backboned the program while The Ink Spots and the Cecil Mack Choir alternated.

Wednesday 4 March 1936
Ella Fitzgerald and the Chick Webb Orchestra broadcast from Radio City with the revamped 'Gems of Color' programme.
Milenberg Joys / *Shine* (vEF)

Friday 6 March 1936
Ella Fitzgerald and the Chick Webb Orchestra play the Sheffield Fraternity Prom (until 7.00am) at Franklin Hall, Yale University in New Haven, Connecticut.

Tuesday 17 March 1936
Ella Fitzgerald records with Teddy Wilson's Orchestra for Brunswick in New York City.
ELLA FITZGERALD (vocal), FRANKIE NEWTON (trumpet), JERRY BLAKE (clarinet/alto sax), TEDDY WILSON (piano), JOHN TRUEHEART (guitar), LENNIE STANFIELD (bass), COZY COLE (drums)
My Melancholy Baby (vEF) / *All My Life* (vEF)
The band also record two instrumentals: *Christopher Columbus* / *I Know That You Know*

Chick Webb and his "Gems of Color" on WJZ any Wednesday evening from 10:30 to 11 o'clock, featuring the melodious voices of Ella Fitzgerald, Charlie Linton, the comedy of Eddie Hunter, the swing string tunes of the Ink Spots and the Mass Voices of Juanita Hall's Choir.

Tuesday 7 April 1936
Ella Fitzgerald records with the Chick Webb Orchestra for Decca in New York City.
ELLA FITZGERALD (vocal), MARIO BAUZA, TAFT JORDAN, BOBBY STARK (trumpets), SANDY WILLIAMS, CLAUDE JONES (trombones), EDGAR SAMPSON (alto sax), PETE CLARK (alto sax), ELMER WILLIAMS (tenor sax), WAYMAN CARVER (tenor sax/flute), DON KIRKPATRICK (piano), JOHN TRUEHEART (guitar), BILL THOMAS (bass), CHICK WEBB (drums)
Love, You're Just A Laugh (vEF) / *Crying My Heart Out For You* (vEF) / *Under The Spell Of The Blues* (vEF) / *When I Get Low I Get High* (vEF)

9 April—Starting Saturday at 4:30pm Chick can be heard until 5:00pm over WEAF. Returning to the same station Wednesday from 5:00pm to 5:30pm.
   On WJZ, as usual, from 10:30 to 11:00pm Chick and his boys will supply the musical background for the "Good Time Party," the same program which once came to us as the "Gems of Color".

Saturday 25 April 1936
Ella Fitzgerald's 18th birthday.

Tuesday 2 June 1936
Ella Fitzgerald records with the Chick Webb Orchestra for Decca in New York City.
ELLA FITZGERALD (vocal), MARIO BAUZA, TAFT JORDAN, BOBBY STARK (trumpets), SANDY WILLIAMS, NAT STORY (trombones), EDGAR SAMPSON (alto sax), PETE CLARK (alto sax), TED McRAE (tenor sax), WAYMAN CARVER (tenor sax/flute), DON KIRKPATRICK (piano), JOHN TRUEHEART (guitar), BILL THOMAS (bass), CHICK WEBB (drums)
Sing Me A Swing Song (And Let Me Dance) (vEF) / *A Little Bit Later On* (vEF) / *Love, You're Just A Laugh* (vEF) / *Devoting My Time To You* (vEF)
The band complete the session with an instrumental: *Go Harlem*

Around the beginning of June, Ella Fitzgerald and the Chick Webb Orchestra wind up their residency at the Savoy Ballroom and set off on a road trip for about six months.

Wednesday 10 June 1936
Ella Fitzgerald and the Chick Webb Orchestra play a dance at East Market Gardens in Akron, Ohio.

Friday 12 June 1936
Ella Fitzgerald and the Chick Webb Orchestra play a Battle of Bands versus the orchestras of Fletcher Henderson, Erskine Tate and Don Redman at the Eighth Regiment Armory in Chicago.

Friday 19 June 1936
Ella Fitzgerald and the Chick Webb Orchestra open a one-week engagement at the Apollo Theatre in New York City. Also on the bill are Pete, Peaches & Duke, the Truckin' Maniacs, Pigmeat Markham, Jimmie Baskette and John Mason.

Thursday 25 June 1936

Ella Fitzgerald and the Chick Webb Orchestra close at the Apollo Theatre in New York City.

Sunday 12 July 1936

Ella Fitzgerald and the Chick Webb Orchestra play a one-nighter opposite the Erskine Tate Orchestra at the Savoy Ballroom in Chicago.

Sunday 19 July 1936

Ella Fitzgerald and the Chick Webb Orchestra play a one-nighter at Tomlinson Hall in Indianapolis, Indiana.

Monday 17 August 1936

Ella Fitzgerald and the Chick Webb Orchestra play a dance at Spanish Gables in Revere Beach, Boston, Massachusetts.

Thursday 20 August 1936

Ella Fitzgerald and the Chick Webb Orchestra play a dance (9.00pm until 2.00am) at the Rainbow Ballroom in Hyannis.

Friday 21 August 1936

Ella Fitzgerald and the Chick Webb Orchestra play a dance at the Roseland Ballroom in Taunton, Massachusetts.

Saturday 12 September 1936

Ella Fitzgerald and the Chick Webb Orchestra appear at the Grand Re-opening of the Savoy Ballroom in New York City after its £50,000 renovation. Also on the bill is Alberto Socarras and his Cuban Orchestra.

Sunday 20 September 1936

Ella Fitzgerald and the Chick Webb Orchestra appear on CBS/NBC radio's 'Intercontinental Concert' (4:00pm to 4:30pm) performing Duke Ellington's *Mood Indigo*. Also appearing are Chief Jesse Cornplanter, the Columbia Symphony Orchestra, the NBC Orchestra, Hal Kemp's Orchestra, and the Fisk Jubilee Singers.

Friday 9 October 1936

Ella Fitzgerald and the Chick Webb Orchestra open a one-week engagement at the Nixon Grand Theatre in Philadelphia. Also on the bill are the Four Ink Spots, Pigmeat Markham, Mason & Baskette, Three Jacks and Madeline Belt.

Thursday 15 October 1936
Ella Fitzgerald and the Chick Webb Orchestra close at the Nixon Grand Theatre in Philadelphia.

Friday 16 October 1936
Ella Fitzgerald and the Chick Webb Orchestra open a one-week engagement at the Apollo Theatre in New York City. Also on the bill are the Four Ink Spots.

Thursday 22 October 1936
Ella Fitzgerald and the Chick Webb Orchestra close at the Apollo Theatre in New York City.

Thursday 29 October 1936
Ella Fitzgerald records with the Chick Webb Orchestra for Decca in New York City.
ELLA FITZGERALD (vocal), MARIO BAUZA, TAFT JORDAN, BOBBY STARK (trumpets), SANDY WILLIAMS, NAT STORY (trombones), LOUIS JORDAN (alto sax), PETE CLARK (alto sax), TED McRAE (tenor sax), WAYMAN CARVER (tenor sax/flute), TOMMY FULFORD (piano), JOHN TRUEHEART (guitar), BEVERLY PEER (bass), CHICK WEBB (drums)
(If You Can't Sing It) You'll Have To Swing It (vEF) / *Swinging On The Reservation* (vEF) / *Spring Fever Blues* (vEF) / *Vote For Mr. Rhythm* (vEF)

Saturday 31 October 1936
Ella Fitzgerald and the Chick Webb Orchestra play a dance at Ricker Gardens in Portland, Maine.

Thursday 5 November 1936
Ella Fitzgerald records with the Benny Goodman Orchestra for Victor in New York City.
ELLA FITZGERALD (vocal), GORDON GRIFFIN, ZEKE ZARCHY, ZIGGY ELMAN (trumpets), RED BALLARD, MURRAY McEACHERN (trombones), BENNY GOODMAN (clarinet), HYMIE SCHERTZER (alto sax), BILL DePEW (alto sax), ARTHUR ROLLINI (tenor sax), VIDO MUSSO (tenor sax), JESS STACY (piano), ALLEN REUSS (guitar), HARRY GOODMAN (bass), GENE KRUPA (drums)
Goodnight, My Love (vEF) / *Take Another Guess* (vEF) / *Did You Mean It?* (vEF)

Tuesday 10 November 1936
Ella Fitzgerald appears on Benny Goodman's coast-to-coast radio show 'Camel Caravan' in New York City. She is back at the Savoy Ballroom for the 12.30 broadcast with Chick:
Memphis Blues / Spring Fever Blues (vEF) / *Go Harlem / Down Home Rag / Vote For Mr Rhythm* (vEF) / *I May Be Wrong / Stop, Look And Listen / Royal Garden Blues / Stompin' At The Savoy* (theme)
During this period Ella has a brief affair with Vido Musso, the Italian tenor sax player with Goodman's band.

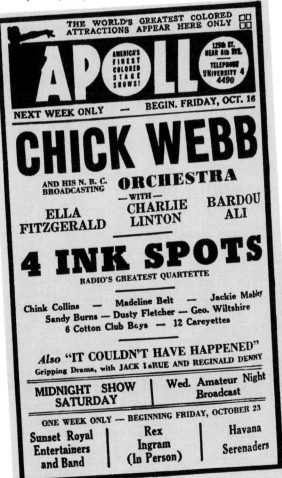

Throughout November and December Ella Fitzgerald and the Chick Webb Orchestra are resident at the Savoy Ballroom in New York City.

Wednesday 11 November 1936
Ella Fitzgerald and the Chick Webb Orchestra broadcast coast-to-coast through WEAF with Irvin S. Cobb's 'Plantation' show in New York City.

Friday 13 November 1936
Ella Fitzgerald and the Chick Webb Orchestra broadcast from the Savoy Ballroom in New York City.
Way Down Yonder In New Orleans / You'll Have To Swing It (vEF) / *Boston Tea Party / Don't Be That Way / When Did You Leave Heaven? / Honeysuckle Rose* (vEF) / *Organ Grinder's Swing / Confessin' / Stompin' At The Savoy* (theme)

Sunday 15 November 1936
Ella Fitzgerald and the Chick Webb Orchestra are joined at the Savoy Ballroom by Lucky Millinder and his Blue Rhythm Band for a one-week engagement.

Wednesday 18 November 1936
Ella Fitzgerald and her Savoy Eight record for Decca in New York City.
ELLA FITZGERALD (vocal), TAFT JORDAN (trumpet), SANDY WILLIAMS (trombone), PETE CLARK (clarinet), TEDDY MCRAE (tenor sax/baritone sax), TOMMY FULFORD (piano), JOHN TRUEHEART (guitar), BEVERLY PEER (bass), CHICK WEBB (drums)
My Last Affair / Organ Grinder's Swing

Thursday 19 November 1936
Ella Fitzgerald and her Savoy Eight again record for Decca in New York City.
Shine / Darktown Strutters' Ball

Saturday 21 November 1936
Lucky Millinder and his Blue Rhythm Band close at the Savoy Ballroom. Ella and Chick stay on.

Saturday 28 November 1936
Ella Fitzgerald and the Chick Webb Orchestra broadcast from the Savoy Ballroom in New York City.
Big John Special / Cryin' My Heart Out (vEF) / *Chief De Sota / I'll Sing You A Thousand Love Songs* (vCL) / *Don't Be That Way / Cream Puff / This Is My Last Affair* (vEF) / *Stompin' At The Savoy*

Thursday 3 December 1936
Ella Fitzgerald and the Chick Webb Orchestra broadcast on Martin Block's 'Make Believe Ballroom' in New York City.
Let's Get Together (theme) / *Clap Hands! Here Comes Charlie / That Man Is Here Again* (vEF) / *Don't Be That Way / Spring Fever Blues* (vEF) / *Honeysuckle Rose* (vEF) / *You'll Have To Swing It* (vEF) / *House Hop / Organ Grinder's Swing* (vEF)

Friday 4 December 1936
Ella Fitzgerald and the Chick Webb Orchestra broadcast from the Savoy Ballroom in New York City.
Jamaica Shout / There's Something In The Air (vEF) / *Riffin' At The Ritz / Love, What Are You Doing To My Heart?* (vCL) / *The Duke Swings Low / I'm An Old Cowhand / Bye Bye Baby / A Little Bit Later On* (vEF) / *Harlem Heat*

Saturday 5 December 1936
Ella Fitzgerald and the Chick Webb Orchestra broadcast from the Savoy Ballroom in New York City.
Henderson Stomp / You're The Only One To Blame (vEF) / *Back Home In Indiana / Milenburg Joys* (vEF) / *Organ Grinder's Swing* (vEF)

Sunday 6 December 1936
Ella Fitzgerald and the Chick Webb Orchestra play opposite Andy Kirk and Billy Hicks at the Savoy Ballroom in New York City.

> Suddenly, in the week 7–11 December, Ella is absent from the Chick Webb band, and she apparently has an abortion. As a result of the operation, Ella is never able to have children.

Sunday 13 December 1936
Ella Fitzgerald and the Chick Webb Orchestra play a Battle of Bands with Tommy Dorsey's Orchestra at the Savoy Ballroom in New York City.

Tuesday 15 December 1936
Ella Fitzgerald and the Chick Webb Orchestra broadcast from NBC Studios (4.15pm) in New York City.
Mr Ghost Goes To Town / In My Seclusion (vCL) / *Harlem Heat / I've Got You Under My Skin / Honeysuckle Rose* (vEF) / *Royal Garden Blues*
At midnight they appear at a Gala Nite Of Stars at the Apollo Theatre. Also billed to appear are Bill Robinson, Ethel Waters, Cab Calloway, Rex Ingram and Pigmeat.

Friday 18 December 1936
Ella Fitzgerald and the Chick Webb Orchestra broadcast from the Savoy Ballroom in New York City.
Facts And Figures / Make Believe Ballroom (vEF) / *It Happens To The Best Of Friends / There's Heaven In My Heart* (vCL) / *Riffin' / Limehouse Blues / My Heart On Fire* (vEF) / *Down Home Rag / Stompin' At The Savoy / Let's Get Together* (theme)

Thursday 31 December 1936
Ella Fitzgerald and the Chick Webb Orchestra play opposite Claude Hopkins and Billy Hicks at the Savoy Ballroom in New York City. At 2.15am they broadcast over WMCA from the Savoy Ballroom.
Let's Get Together (theme) / *House Hop / Until The Real Thing Comes Along* (vEF,CL) / *Jam Session / Love, What Are You Doing To My Heart?* (vCL) / *Mr. Ghost Goes To Town / Copenhagen / This Is My Last Affair* (vEF) / *Bugle Call Rag*

1937

Friday 1 January 1937
Ella Fitzgerald and the Chick Webb Orchestra play opposite Claude Hopkins and Billy Hicks at the Savoy Ballroom (3.00pm until 3.00am) in New York City.

Tuesday 5 January 1937
Ella Fitzgerald and the Chick Webb Orchestra broadcast from the Savoy Ballroom (4.00pm),
Vote For Mr Rhythm (vEF) / *Jamboree* / *Darling, Not Without You* (vCL) / *Swing Your Feet* / *Blue Lou* / *You Turned The Tables On Me* (vEF) / *Way Down Yonder In New Orleans* / *House Hop* / *There's Something In The Air* (vEF) / *Let's Get Together* (theme) and again at midnight: *That's Life I Guess* (vEF) / *Big Chief De Sota* / *Together We Live* (vLJ) / *Cream Puff* / *Sing Me A Swing Song* (vEF) / *Limehouse Blues* / *Reservation* (vEF)

Wednesday 6 January 1937
Ella Fitzgerald broadcasts on WMCA's 'Let's Listen to Lucidin' from the Biltmore Hotel in New York City, accompanied by Stuff Smith's Lucidin Orchestra featuring trumpeter Jonah Jones.
Did You Mean It? / *Take Another Guess* / *Goodnight My Love*

> Helen Ward's illness, which kept her off the commercial with "Stuff" Smith and his band, gave Ella Fitzgerald the break of her lifetime...

Friday 8 January 1937
Ella Fitzgerald broadcasts on WMCA's 'Let's Listen to Lucidin' from the Biltmore Hotel, accompanied by Stuff Smith and his Lucidin Orchestra: *Copper Colored Gal*

Tuesday 12 January 1937
Ella Fitzgerald and the Chick Webb Orchestra broadcast from the Savoy Ballroom (4.00pm)
Honeysuckle Rose (vEF) / *Swinging For The King* / *Living In Seclusion* (vLJ) / *Stompin' At The Savoy* / *There's Frost On The Moon* (vEF,CL) / *Tain't Good* (vEF) / *Harlem Heat* / *Swingin' On The Reservation* (vEF) / *Let's Get Together* (theme)

Thursday 14 January 1937
Ella Fitzgerald records with the Chick Webb Orchestra for Decca in New York City.
ELLA FITZGERALD (vocal), MARIO BAUZA, TAFT JORDAN, BOBBY STARK (trumpets), SANDY WILLIAMS, NAT STORY (trombones), LOUIS JORDAN (alto sax), PETE CLARK (alto sax), TED MCRAE (tenor sax), WAYMAN CARVER (tenor sax/flute), TOMMY FULFORD (piano), JOHN TRUEHEART (guitar), BEVERLY PEER (bass), CHICK WEBB (drums)
Take Another Guess (vEF) / *Love Marches On* (vEF,LJ,CL)
At the same session Ella records with The Mills Brothers:
ELLA FITZGERALD, THE MILLS BROTHERS (vocal), BERNARD ADDISON (guitar): *Big Boy Blue*

Friday 15 January 1937
Ella Fitzgerald broadcasts on WMCA's 'Let's Listen to Lucidin' from the Biltmore Hotel, accompanied by Stuff Smith and his Lucidin Orchestra: *Oh Say, Can You Swing?* / *It's De-Lovely* / *In The Chapel In The Moonlight*
Ella Fitzgerald and the Chick Webb Orchestra record for Decca in New York City.
There's Frost On The Moon (vEF,LJ,CL) / *Gee, But You're Swell* (vLJ)

> January 16—The Good Time Society last week made its debut on a coast-to-coast hook-up, featuring Chick Webb and his Band, Ella Fitzgerald, Taft Jordan, the Juanita Hall Choir, supported by sixteen mixed voices, and the Four Ink Spots, over WJZ at 10:00pm. The show is on the air every Monday, 10–10:30pm over the Blue Network coast-to-coast on WJZ.

Monday 18 January 1937
Ella Fitzgerald broadcasts on WMCA's 'Let's Listen to Lucidin' from the Biltmore Hotel in New York City.
That Man Is Here Again / *In The Chapel In The Moonlight*

Friday 22 January 1937
Ella Fitzgerald and the Chick Webb Orchestra open a one-week engagement at the Apollo Theatre (*below*) in New York City. Also on the bill are George McGlennon, Pigmeat Markham, Anise & Aland, Maud Russell and Babe Wallace.

Wednesday 27 January 1937
Ella Fitzgerald and the Chick Webb Orchestra broadcast from the Apollo Theatre in New York City.
Spring Fever Blues (vEF) / *There's Frost On The Moon* (vEF,CL,LJ)

Thursday 28 January 1937
Ella Fitzgerald and the Chick Webb Orchestra close at the Apollo Theatre in New York City.

Saturday 30 January 1937
Ella Fitzgerald and the Chick Webb Orchestra broadcast from the Savoy Ballroom in New York City.
Stompin' At The Savoy (theme) / *Goodnight, My Love* (vEF) / *Blue Lou* / *One Never Knows, Does One?* (vCL) / *Swingin' For The King* / *Swingin' On The Reservation* (vEF)

Wednesday 3 February 1937
Ella Fitzgerald and The Mills Brothers record for Decca in New York City.
ELLA FITZGERALD, THE MILLS BROTHERS (vocal), BERNARD ADDISON (guitar)
Dedicated To You

Friday 5 February 1937
Ella Fitzgerald and the Chick Webb Orchestra broadcast live to England for the BBC on a show called 'America Dances–Swing Music No.2'.
Royal Garden Blues / *Honeysuckle Rose* / *Somebody Loves Me* / *Spring Fever Blues* (vEF) / *There's Something In The Air* (vEF)

Monday 8 February 1937
Ella Fitzgerald and the Chick Webb Orchestra record radio transcriptions for Radio WJZ at Radio City in New York City.
Vote For Mr Rhythm (vEF) / *Big Boy Blue* (vEF)

Friday 12 February 1937
Chick Webb takes part in a jam session with Benny Goodman and Teddy Wilson at the Scottsboro Herndon Ball at the Savoy Ballroom in New York City.

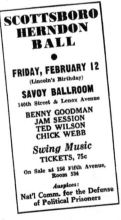

SCOTTSBORO
HERNDON
BALL
●
FRIDAY, FEBRUARY 12
(Lincoln's Birthday)
SAVOY BALLROOM
140th Street & Lenox Avenue
BENNY GOODMAN
JAM SESSION
TED WILSON
CHICK WEBB
Swing Music
TICKETS, 75c
On Sale at 156 Fifth Avenue,
Room 534
Auspices:
Nat'l Comm. for the Defense
of Political Prisoners

Saturday 13 February 1937
Ella Fitzgerald, Chick Webb, Teddy McRae, Taft Jordan and Tommy Fulford are guests on CBS Saturday Night Swing Session broadcast (6.45–7.15pm).
Spring Fever Blues (vEF) / *This Is My Last Affair* (vEF) Chick and McRae also back Bunny Berigan on *Formal Night In Harlem*

Wednesday 17 February 1937
Ella Fitzgerald and the Chick Webb Orchestra play a Benefit Ball for New York flood victims at the Alhambra Ballroom in New York City. Also appearing are the bands of Cab Calloway and Edgar Hayes.

Friday 19 February 1937
Ella Fitzgerald is awarded the key to the city of Yonkers in a ceremony at the Polish Community Center in Yonkers, NY. Ella, Chick and the band play for the Paradise Boys' Club at the Center.
A March of Time film is released on this day featuring an all-too-brief clip of the band performing at the Savoy Ballroom.

PARADISE BOYS' CLUB
FEATURES
ELLA FITZGERALD
AND A COMPLETE FLOOR SHOW FROM HARLEM
At the
POLISH COMMUNITY CENTER
58 WAVERLY STREET, YONKERS, N.Y.
Friday Night, February 19, 1937
ADMISSION 75 CENTS
Table Reservation $1.00   For Table: Phone Yonkers 2546-M

Mayor Loehr Presents
Key of City to Girl

1,200 Attend an Affair Given for Popular Swing Singer

Honored

More than 1,200 persons were present at the Polish Community Center, Yonkers, last Friday evening to see Mayor Joseph Loehr give Ella Fitzgerald the key to the city. As early as seven o'clock automobiles from various points in the county commenced to file into the Hilly City.

Miss Fitzgerald, who was reared in Yonkers, was highly praised by Mayor Loehr. "We're mighty proud of Ella's achievements," he said, "and we wish her the very best of success."

John Lee, one of the officials of the Paradise Boys' Club, sponsors of the dance, also introduced City Judge Martin Bray Assemblyman William Doran and Commissioner of Public Works Edward Murray.

Lester Carter, proprietor of the Log Cabin, Nepperhan, where Ella once crooned, was also on hand to cheer for her. "I knew that she was going to make the grade," Mr. Carter said. "She always had that certain swing quality that grips you."

Ella Takes Floor.

After several speakers had showered Ella with congratulations, the singer thanked those present for the honors "that had been bestowed upon her," and promised to do her utmost to maintain their admiration.

Lester Kingsland, president of the Paradise Boys; Ralph West, Carleton Seymour, John Lee, Leon Middleton and the rest of the organization's members were the recipients of the audience's plaudits when they were introduced.

Miss Fitzgerald is now featured with Chick Webb and his chicks and is well known for her radio work and recordings.

ELLA FITZGERALD, popular swing singer, who was honored Friday at a dance given for her by the Paradise Boys of Yonkers.

CHICK WEBB RECEIVES 5000 LETTERS A WEEK
New York, N.Y.—Chick Webb and his orchestra, featured on the NBC sustaining program, Good Time Society, receive an average of 5,000 fan letters a week... Starting March 8th, the program will be broadcast over Station WJZ and the NBC network at 9 P.M., Monday nights.

Saturday 20 February 1937
Ella Fitzgerald and the Chick Webb Orchestra broadcast from the Savoy Ballroom (11.30pm) in New York City.
Stompin' At The Savoy (theme) / *Sugar Foot Stomp* / *You'll Have To Swing It* (vEF) / *Stop, Look And Listen* / *You're Laughin' At Me* (vLJ) / *Jangled Nerves* / *Feelin' Low* (vEF) / *Swingin' On The Reservation* (vEF)

Tuesday 23 February 1937
Ella Fitzgerald and the Chick Webb Orchestra broadcast from the Savoy Ballroom (4.15pm)
Facts And Figures / *You Showed Me The Way* (vEF) / *Easy To Love* / *Swinging Along* / *The Mayor Of Alabam'* (vLJ) / *Rusty Hinge* / *Goodnight, My Love* (vEF) / *That's A-Plenty*

Sunday 28 February 1937
The Chick Webb and Fletcher Henderson Orchestras engage in a Battle of the Bands at the Savoy Ballroom.

Monday 1 March 1937
Ella and the Chick Webb Orchestra broadcast with the Four Ink Spots from the studio (10pm) in New York City.
I Found A New Baby / Swing, Mr Charlie (v4IS) / *What Will I Tell My Heart?* (vEF) / *Oh Dear, What Can The Matter Be? / You Showed Me The Way* (vEF) / *Cross Patch* (v4IS) / *Stompin' At The Savoy*

Friday 5 March 1937
Ella and the Chick Webb Orchestra broadcast from the Savoy Ballroom (11.45pm) in New York City.
The Goona Goo (vEF) / *Love Is The Thing, So They Say* (vEF) / *House Hop*

Sunday 7 March 1937
The Chick Webb and Duke Ellington Orchestras engage in a Battle of the Bands at the Savoy Ballroom.

Friday 12 March 1937
Ella Fitzgerald and the Chick Webb Orchestra play a Kiddies Welcome Ball at Krueger's Auditorium in Newark, N.J.

Sunday 14 March 1937
Ella Fitzgerald and Chick Webb attend an afternoon jam session at the new Master Recording Studios in New York City. The session is produced by Helen Oakley for Irving Mills to launch the Master and Variety record labels. Duke Ellington, Artie Shaw, Frankie Newton, Mezz Mezzrow, George Wettling and Eddie Condon are among others taking part. Ella is a big hit and sings four tunes, accompanied by Duke Ellington, Rex Stewart and Chick Webb.

Lots of swell music was made during the party. Basie's rhythm section started things off, joined by various reeds and brass, achieving at times a colossal drive. Benny Goodman and Chick Webb joined forces while Ella Fitzgerald sang three fast songs; Artie Shaw and George Wettling impressed everybody, and Duke along with Rex Stewart, Harry Carney and a few others of his virtuosi, literally panicked the folk late in the day.

Friday 19 March 1937
Ella and the Chick Webb Orchestra broadcast from the Savoy Ballroom (11.45pm) in New York City.
You Showed Me The Way (vEF) / *Down Home Rag / Stompin' At The Savoy*

Tuesday 23 March 1937
Ella and the Chick Webb Orchestra broadcast from the Savoy Ballroom in New York City.
I Got A Guy (vEF) / *Memphis Blues / Someday, Sweetheart* (vCL) / *Honeysuckle Rose / House Hop / Let's Get Together* (theme)

Wednesday 24 March 1937
Ella Fitzgerald records with the Chick Webb Orchestra for Decca in New York City.
ELLA FITZGERALD (vocal), MARIO BAUZA, TAFT JORDAN, BOBBY STARK (trumpets), SANDY WILLIAMS, NAT STORY (trombones), LOUIS JORDAN (alto sax), PETE CLARK (alto sax), TED MCRAE (tenor sax), WAYMAN CARVER (tenor sax/flute), TOMMY FULFORD (piano), JOHN TRUEHEART (guitar), BEVERLY PEER (bass), CHICK WEBB (drums)
You Showed Me The Way (vEF) / *Cryin' Mood* (vEF) / *Love Is The Thing, So They Say* (vEF) / *Wake Up And Live* (vEF & trio)
The band also record tracks without Ella: *Rusty Hinge* (vLJ) / *It's Swell Of You* (vLJ) / *Clap Hands, Here Comes Charley / That Naughty Waltz*

Thursday 25 March 1937
Chick Webb records with the Gotham Stompers in New York City. The all-star group features members of the Duke Ellington band including Ivie Anderson.

Friday 26 March 1937
Ella Fitzgerald and the Chick Webb Orchestra open a one-week engagement at the Howard Theatre in Washington, D.C.

Thursday 1 April 1937
Ella Fitzgerald and the Chick Webb Orchestra close at the Howard Theatre in Washington, D.C.

Friday 2 April 1937
Ella Fitzgerald and the Chick Webb Orchestra open a one-week engagement at the Nixon Grand Theatre in Philadelphia.

Saturday 3 April 1937
Ella Fitzgerald and the Chick Webb Orchestra broadcast from the Nixon Grand Theatre in Philadelphia.
Sugar Foot Stomp / I Can't Break The Habit Of You (vEF) / *Thou Swell / Charmaine* (vCL) / *Swing Low, Sweet Chariot / The Mayor Of Alabam' / Clap Hands, Here Comes Charlie / Let's Get Together* (theme)

Thursday 8 April 1937
Ella Fitzgerald and the Chick Webb Orchestra close at the Nixon Grand Theatre in Philadelphia.

Friday 9 April 1937
In the afternoon Ella, Chick and the band give a performance for children at the New York Colored Orphan Asylum in Yonkers, New York.
In the evening, Ella Fitzgerald and the Chick Webb Orchestra open a one-week engagement at the Apollo Theatre in New York City. Also on the bill are Henri Wessels, Cook & Brown, White's Lindy-Maniacs, Hilda Perleno, Pigmeat Markham, John Mason, Jimmie Baskette and Wolford's Pets.

CHICK WEBB TO TOUR
Chick Webb and his orchestra, famed colored radio, recording and dance band, are being set for a one night stand tour by Consolidated Radio Artists, Inc.

Thursday 15 April 1937
Ella Fitzgerald and the Chick Webb Orchestra close at the Apollo Theatre in New York City.

Friday 16 April 1937
Ella Fitzgerald and the Chick Webb Orchestra play a prom dance for Holly Cross College at the Bancroft Hotel Ballroom in Worcester, Massachusetts.

Saturday 24 April 1937
Ella Fitzgerald and the Chick Webb Orchestra play a dance at the Old Orchard Pier in Old Orchard Beach, Portland, Maine.

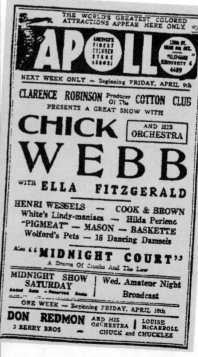

Left: Chick and Ella on stage at the Apollo Theatre.

Sunday 25 April 1937
Ella Fitzgerald's 19th birthday.

Monday 26 April 1937
Ella Fitzgerald and the Chick Webb Orchestra play a dance (9.00pm until 2.00am) at the Lincoln Colonnade in Washington, D.C.

Tuesday 4 May 1937
Ella Fitzgerald and the Chick Webb Orchestra play a dance at the Palais Royal in Philadelphia.

Tuesday 11 May 1937
Ella Fitzgerald and the Chick Webb Orchestra battle with the Benny Goodman Orchestra at the Savoy Ballroom in New York City.

Ace Swing Bands in Battle of Jazz

Generating sepia rhythm, Chick Webb and his famous swing band will strive to outblaze Benny Goodman's white heat, when America's foremost dance orchestras tangle at the Savoy Ballroom Tuesday night, May 11. The terrific rivalry that has been steamed up between the band leaders should be settled once and for all when they cross musical weapons before the largest crowd that has witnessed a swing battle.

Chick Webb, who had been considered supreme in the field of swing music until the peership was challenged by the arrival of Benny Goodman on the musical horizon, when the latter augmented his aggregation with Teddy Wilson and Lionel Hampton, two of America's outstanding artists, will defend his swing crown.

There was an incredible sight on Lenox Avenue and 140th Street Tuesday, May 11. Mounted police, the fire department, deputy inspectors, and a score of ordinary cops were required to keep in check a mob of ten thousand souls who were fighting to get into the Savoy Ballroom to hear the battle of the century between Benny Goodman and Chick Webb's orchestras. About four thousand people actually managed to jam their way into the Savoy, where four or five cops were stationed on the Goodman bandstand to maintain law and order.

It was another case where expectations were too high, for Benny's band was obviously flustered by the proceedings. The noise level was so high that none but the brass soloists was even audible; the p.a. system further complicated matters by refusing to function from time to time. Consequently, the band tried a bit too hard, and, although they were well liked by the crowd, Chick Webb actually walked off with the honors (an opinion shared by Benny himself). Although Chick's band indulged in much jive, they actually played better than I have heard them in ages, helped enormously by Ella Fitzgerald and Chick's spectacular drumming. Chick placed himself and his drums right in front of his band, while poor Gene was buried in a back row, invisible to the audience because of the formidable cops who stood up in front of him.

Right: Gene Krupa works up a sweat trying to compete with Chick.

Saturday 15 May 1937
Ella Fitzgerald and the Chick Webb Orchestra broadcast over WJZ (2:30pm) from the Savoy Ballroom in New York City.
What A Shuffle! / I Can't Break The Habit Of You (vEF) / *Take It From The Top / Where Are You?* (vCL) / *I Found A New Baby / Rusty Hinge / There's A Lull In My Life* (vEF) / *That's A-Plenty / Caravan / Let's Get Together* (theme)
In the evening, they again broadcast (WMCA, 11:30pm) from the Savoy Ballroom.
Jam Session / Holiday In Harlem (vEF) / *The Naughty Waltz / Charmaine / Take It From The Top / Clap Hands, Here Comes Charlie / So They Say* (vEF) / *Copenhagen*

Friday 21 May 1937
Ella Fitzgerald and the Chick Webb Orchestra broadcast over WMCA (11:40pm) from the Savoy Ballroom in New York City.
You Showed Me The Way (vEF) / *Blue Lou / Thou Swell / Dedicated To You* (vEF) / *When You And I Were Young, Maggie / Let's Get Together* (theme)

Saturday 22 May 1937
Ella Fitzgerald and the Chick Webb Orchestra broadcast over WJZ (3:00pm) from the Savoy Ballroom in New York City.
Memphis Blues / I've Got Rain In My Eyes (vEF) / *Jamaica Shout / Holiday In Harlem* (vEF) / *Copenhagen / Stompin' At The Savoy / Harlem Congo / I'm In A Crying Mood* (vEF) / *Jam Session / Let's Get Together* (theme)
Ella Fitzgerald and the Chick Webb Orchestra broadcast over WMCA (11:30pm) from the Savoy Ballroom.
Go Harlem / There's A Lull In My Life (vEF) / *September In The Rain* (vCL) / *I Found A New Baby / Mayor Of Alabam'* (vLJ) / *Big John Special / You Showed Me The Way* (vEF) / *Chick Webb Stomp*

Monday 24 May 1937
Ella Fitzgerald and her Savoy Eight again record for Decca in New York City.
ELLA FITZGERALD (vocal), TAFT JORDAN (trumpet), SANDY WILLIAMS (trombone), LOUIS JORDAN (alto sax), TEDDY MCRAE (tenor sax/baritone sax), TOMMY FULFORD (piano), BOBBY JOHNSON (guitar), BEVERLY PEER (bass), CHICK WEBB (drums)
All Over Nothing At All / If You Ever Should Leave / Everyone's Wrong But Me / Deep In The Heart Of The South
Ella Fitzgerald and the Chick Webb Orchestra broadcast on NBC's 'Goodtime Society' (11:0pm) in New York City.
I've Got A Dime (vEF) / *Caravan / Whoa, Babe* (vEF) / *?*

Friday 28 May 1937

Ella Fitzgerald and the Chick Webb Orchestra play a Iota Phi Lamba Sorority Dance at the Savoy Ballroom in New York City.

Sunday 30 May 1937

Ella Fitzgerald and the Chick Webb Orchestra play a Decoration Day dance at the East Market Gardens in Akron, Ohio.

Thursday 10 June 1937

Ella Fitzgerald and the Chick Webb Orchestra play an Annual Commencement Prom (9.00pm until 2.00am) at the Memorial Hall in Dayton, Ohio. The Noble Sissle Orchestra is also featured in a Battle of Music.

Saturday 12 June 1937

Ella Fitzgerald and the Chick Webb Orchestra play a dance (9.00pm until 2.00am) at the Vanity Fair Ballroom in Huntington, West Virginia.

Monday 14 June 1937

Ella Fitzgerald and the Chick Webb Orchestra play a dance (9.00pm until 3.00am) at the Graystone Gardens in Detroit, Michigan.

Friday 18 June 1937

Ella Fitzgerald and the Chick Webb Orchestra open a one-week engagement at the Regal Theatre in Chicago.

Thursday 24 June 1937

Ella Fitzgerald and the Chick Webb Orchestra close at the Regal Theatre in Chicago.

Monday 3 July 1937

Ella Fitzgerald and the Chick Webb Orchestra resume their broadcasting schedule on WJZ's 'Good Time Society' from New York City.

Chick Webb, his Savoy swing orchestra and Ella Fitzgerald, after a hurried trip from the West was again over the national hook up of WJZ Monday night, featuring the entertainment of the "Good Time Society." It's rumored that Webb is being considered by a commercial sponsor.

Sunday 4 July 1937

Ella Fitzgerald and the Chick Webb Orchestra play a concert (11.00pm until midnight) followed by a dance (until 4.00am) at the Roseland Ballroom in Taunton, Massachusetts.

Webb's Band in Sour Groove

Chick Webb arrived a good two hours late when his band played the Revere Nautical Gardens. A very disappointing performance until Chick showed up with a ticket for speeding. He worked hard the rest of the night but the band was in that sour groove and stayed there.

Wednesday 7 July 1937

Ella Fitzgerald and the Chick Webb Orchestra play a dance (until 1.00am) at the Nautical Plaza in Revere, Massachusetts.

Friday 9 July 1937

Ella Fitzgerald and the Chick Webb Orchestra play a dance at the Bal-a-l'air in Worcester, Massachusetts.

Sunday 11 July 1937

Ella Fitzgerald and the Chick Webb Orchestra play a dance at the Villa Casanova in South Plains, New Jersey.

Monday 12 July 1937

Ella Fitzgerald and the Chick Webb Orchestra broadcast on WJZ's 'Good Time Society' (8.00pm) from Radio City in New York City: *What A Shuffle* / *If You Ever Should Leave* (vEF) / *I Never Knew* / *Stop! You're Breaking My Heart* (vEF) / *Clap Hands! Here Comes Charlie*

Wednesday 14 July 1937

Ella Fitzgerald and the Chick Webb Orchestra play a dance at Carlin's Ballroom in Baltimore, Maryland.

Thursday 15 July 1937

Ella Fitzgerald and the Chick Webb Orchestra play a dance at the Bayshore Pavilion in Hampton, Virginia.

Wednesday 21 July 1937

Ella Fitzgerald and the Chick Webb Orchestra play a dance at the Sunset Gardens in Atlanta, Georgia. The crowd of 2100 breaks all previous attendance records.

Sunday 25 July 1937

Ella Fitzgerald and the Chick Webb Orchestra play a dance at the Pelican Dance Hall in New Orleans, La.

July 31: Chick Webb Orchestra will not appear on the weekly (Monday) 'Good Time Society' program until September. They have been replaced by Willie Bryant.

Friday 6 August 1937

Ella Fitzgerald and the Chick Webb Orchestra play a one-nighter in Fort Worth, Texas.

Saturday 7 August 1937

Ella Fitzgerald and the Chick Webb Orchestra appear at the Pan-American Exposition in Dallas, Texas. Between 8.30 and 9.30pm they give a free performance for whites only in the Amphitheatre band shell. At 10.00pm they move to the Agricultural Hall to play a dance for blacks only. At the dance there is a section reserved for white spectators, but without dancing privileges. Next day, the band head north on a series of one-nighters through Oklahoma (Muskogee, Oklahoma City, Tulsa) and Mississippi (Greenville).

Wednesday 18 August 1937

Ella Fitzgerald and the Chick Webb Orchestra play a dance (9.00pm–2.00am) at the Armory in Asbury Park, New Jersey.

Thursday 19 August 1937

Ella Fitzgerald and the Chick Webb Orchestra open a one-week engagement at Loew's State Theatre in New York City. Also on the bill are Chuck & Chuckles, Collins & Peterson, Gwynne and Brown & Ames. The movie is 'Easy Living' starring Jean Arthur, Edward Arnold and Ray Milland.

Saturday 21 August 1937

Teenage fan Bob Inman sees the 4.15pm show at Loew's State Theatre in New York City.
Let's Get Together (theme) / *Harlem Congo* / *I Ought To Have My Head Examined* (vLJ) / *September In The Rain* (vCL) / *King Porter Stomp* / *Sweet Sue* (quintet) / *There's A Lull In My Life* (vEF) / *Royal Garden Blues* (Ella leading the band)

Wednesday 25 August 1937

Ella Fitzgerald and the Chick Webb Orchestra close at Loew's State Theatre in New York City.

Friday 27 August 1937

Ella Fitzgerald and the Chick Webb Orchestra play a dance (until 1.00am) at Canobie Lake Park in Salem, N.H. Part of the proceedings are broadcast over WHDH.

Let's Get Together (theme) / *Clap Hands! Here Comes Charlie* / *You Showed Me The Way* (vEF) / *When You And I Were Young, Maggie* / *September In The Rain* (vCL) / *Big John Special* / *Chick Webb Stomp* / *Sugar Foot Stomp*

Tuesday 31 August 1937

Ella Fitzgerald and the Chick Webb Orchestra play a dance at the Roseland Ballroom in Taunton, Massachusetts.

Wednesday 1 September 1937

Ella Fitzgerald and the Chick Webb Orchestra play a dance at Kimball's Starlight Ballroom in Boston, Massachusetts.

Friday 3 September 1937

Ella Fitzgerald and the Chick Webb Orchestra open a one-week engagement at the Apollo Theatre in New York City. Also on the bill are Babe Wallace, Norman Blake, Sonny & Helen, Billie Lucky, Boots & Saddles, Gallic, George & Monte and the 16 Harperettes.

Saturday 4 September 1937

Ella Fitzgerald and the Chick Webb Quintet broadcast on CBS' Saturday Night Swing Club in New York City.

Sweet Sue (quintet) / *In A Little Spanish Town* (quintet) / *Swing, Brother, Swing* (vEF with CBS band)

Ella Fitzgerald "Stuck" In Elevator

New York, N.Y.—Ella Fitzgerald, swing songstress, recently had high hopes nearly dashed. She rushed into an elevator to make a CBS "Swing Club" broadcast with but four minutes to spare. Somewhere between floors, the car stuck. With no time and in no mood to wait for repairs, Ella demanded action. The trap at the top of the cage was opened and 220 pounds of songstress started through. It took three helpers from above and most of the elevator inmates below to enable the husky singer to make the studio with just ten seconds to spare.

Wednesday 8 September 1937

Ella Fitzgerald and the Chick Webb Orchestra broadcast over WMCA on Amateur Hour from the Apollo Theatre in New York City.

Strictly Jive / *Shine* (vEF) / *I May Be Wrong* (program theme)

Thursday 9 September 1937

Ella Fitzgerald and the Chick Webb Orchestra close at the Apollo Theatre in New York City.

Friday 10 September 1937

Ella Fitzgerald and the Chick Webb Orchestra play a dance at Canobie Lake Park in Salem, New Hampshire.

Monday 13 September 1937

Ella Fitzgerald and the Chick Webb Orchestra play a dance at Kimball's Starlight Ballroom in Boston, Massachusetts.

Thursday 16 September 1937

Ella Fitzgerald and the Chick Webb Orchestra open a one-week engagement at Loew's State Theatre in New York City. Also on the bill are Sid Marion, Mark Plant and Bert Nagle & Girls. The movie presentation is 'Topper' starring Constance Bennett and Cary Grant.

Wednesday 22 September 1937

Ella Fitzgerald and the Chick Webb Orchestra close at Loew's State Theatre in New York City.

Friday 24 September 1937

Ella Fitzgerald and the Chick Webb Orchestra open a one-week engagement at the Howard Theatre in Washington, D.C.

Thursday 30 September 1937

Ella Fitzgerald and the Chick Webb Orchestra close at the Howard Theatre in Washington, D.C.

Friday 1 October 1937
Ella Fitzgerald and the Chick Webb Orchestra open a one-week engagement at the Royal Theatre in Baltimore, Maryland. Also on the bill are the 6 Ubangi Boys and Conway & Parks.

Thursday 7 October 1937
Ella Fitzgerald and the Chick Webb Orchestra close at the Royal Theatre in Baltimore, Maryland.

Monday 11 October 1937
Ella Fitzgerald and the Chick Webb Orchestra play a dance (9.00pm until 2.00am) at the Worcester Auditorium in Worcester, Massachusetts.

Tuesday 12 October 1937
Ella Fitzgerald and the Chick Webb Orchestra play a one-nighter at the Commodore in Lowell, Massachusetts.

Wednesday 13 October 1937
Ella Fitzgerald and the Chick Webb Orchestra play a one-nighter at Ricker Gardens in Portland, Maine.

Thursday 14 October 1937
Ella Fitzgerald and the Chick Webb Orchestra play a dance at the Roseland Ballroom in Taunton, Massachusetts.

Sunday 17 October 1937
Ella Fitzgerald and the Chick Webb Orchestra return to their residency at the Savoy Ballroom in New York City.

Saturday 23 October 1937
Ella Fitzgerald and Chick Webb appear on 'Saturday Night Swing Session' radio show (7.00pm) at CBS in New York City.
If It's The Last Thing I Do (vEF with CBS Orch) / *Clap Hands! Here Comes Charlie* (Chick Webb with CBS Orch) / *Rock It For Me* (vEF with CBS Orch)
After the show they travel back uptown to the Savoy.

Rivals? Why Ethel Gave Ella Her Biggest Thrill!

Ethel Waters gave Ella Fitzgerald the biggest thrill of her singing career!

Ella says so herself, and this ought to clear up for all time any question of whether the two are rivals for the title of having first brounght swing to the world.

It was at the Apollo Theatre about a month ago that I got my biggest thrill, Ella said.

Miss Waters came back stage and told me that my voice was "so refreshing" and that it was 'something different? Those were her exact words, and I shall never forget them or the way she said them."

But how about that story that Miss Waters told a Harlem audience that she was singing swing just as it is sung now twenty years ago, she was asked? Ella is only twenty-two now.

"Oh that," she laughed, "well, believe it or not, the first I knew of that was when I read it in the papers, and I don't know yet what it was all about."

She has had some other thrilling moments, too. For instance, I told her I remembered well the first night that I heard her on the radio night— the night that Benny Goodman introduced her on the Camel hour, explaining that he usually went down to Harlem, trying to find talent, and that Ella Fitzgerald was the best thing he's ever seen.

"I remember it well, too, and always will," she declared. I was so thrilled!

"We had been playing at the Savoy and Benny Goodman often came in, and came back to talk to us, but when he asked if I'd come up to Radio City and be his guest on the Camel hour, I nearly swooned."

Then, the other day, she had her first airplane ride, when the band took a chartered plane out of Washington to make a Newark, N.J. engagement.

The pilot had cautioned her that she might be air sick, but she landed as good as she started, she said.

"I was afraid to go at first," Ella said. "They didn't tell me until the last moment that we had to go by plane and I was rushed and excited and scared all at one and the same time, but after we took off, it proved great fun."

Sunday 24 October 1937

Ella Fitzgerald and the Chick Webb Quintet appear on WNEW's Sunday Night Swing Concert (11.30pm until midnight) in New York City.

Swing, Brother, Swing (vEF) / *In A Little Spanish Town* (Chick Webb Quintet)

Wednesday 27 October 1937

Ella Fitzgerald records with the Chick Webb Orchestra for Decca in New York City.

ELLA FITZGERALD (vocal), MARIO BAUZA, TAFT JORDAN, BOBBY STARK (trumpets), SANDY WILLIAMS, NAT STORY (trombones), LOUIS JORDAN (alto sax), CHAUNCEY HAUGHTON (clarinet/alto sax), TED MCRAE (tenor sax), WAYMAN CARVER (tenor sax/flute), TOMMY FULFORD (piano), BOBBY JOHNSON (guitar), BEVERLY PEER (bass), CHICK WEBB (drums)

Just A Simple Melody (vEF) / *I Got A Guy* (vEF) / *Holiday In Harlem* (vEF)

The band also records an instrumental: *Strictly Jive*

Friday 29 October 1937

Celebrity Night at the Savoy Ballroom features Ella Fitzgerald and the Chick Webb Orchestra plus the Teddy Hill Orchestra and the Savoy Sultans.

Sunday 31 October 1937

Ella And the Chick Webb Quintet appear at a Sunday Morning Swing Concert at the International Casino in New York. Erskine Hawkins is also a guest. part of the concert is broadcast at 11.30am over WNEW.

Swing, Brother, Swing (vEF) / *In A Little Spanish Town* (Quintet)

Halloween Rag-a-Muffin Ball at the Savoy Ballroom features Ella Fitzgerald and the Chick Webb Orchestra plus the Savoy Sultans. Teenage swing fan Bob Inman is there and remembers: '*Just A Simple Melody* (recorded last week for Decca with Ella Fitzgerald) and *Clap Hands! Here Comes Charlie* were the two outstanding numbers.' Ella signs for Bob:

Monday 1 November 1937

Ella Fitzgerald records with the Chick Webb Orchestra for Decca in New York City.

Rock It For Me (vEF)

The band also records two instrumentals: *Squeeze Me / Harlem Congo*

A small group from the band, Chick Webb and his Little Chicks, also record at this session: *Sweet Sue, Just You*

Tuesday 2 November 1937

Ella Fitzgerald records with the Chick Webb Orchestra for Decca in New York City.

ELLA FITZGERALD (vocal), MARIO BAUZA, TAFT JORDAN, BOBBY STARK (trumpets), SANDY WILLIAMS, NAT STORY (trombones), LOUIS JORDAN (alto sax), CHAUNCEY HAUGHTON (clarinet/alto sax), TED MCRAE (tenor sax), WAYMAN CARVER (tenor sax/flute), TOMMY FULFORD (piano), BOBBY JOHNSON (guitar), BEVERLY PEER (bass), CHICK WEBB (drums)

I Want To Be Happy (vEF)

The band also records an instrumental: *Hallelujah!*

Wednesday 3 November 1937

Ella Fitzgerald and the Chick Webb Orchestra close at the Savoy Ballroom in New York City to undertake another midwest tour.

Thursday 4 November 1937

Ella Fitzgerald and the Chick Webb Orchestra open a one-week engagement at the RKO Theatre in Boston. Also on the bill are Peg Leg Bates and Buck & Bubbles.

Wednesday 10 November 1937

Ella Fitzgerald and the Chick Webb Orchestra close at the RKO Theatre in Boston.

Saturday 13 November 1937

Ella Fitzgerald and the Chick Webb Orchestra open a one-week engagement at the Palace Theatre in Chicago.

Webb Has Good Week at Palace Theatre

Chicago, Illinois—Chick Webb brought his swing band into the RKO-Palace here for a week in November, added Ella Fitzgerald to the show. Attendance records at the Palace were broken during his stay.

Monday 15 November 1937

Ella Fitzgerald and the Chick Webb Orchestra play a Battle of Bands with Jimmy Dorsey's Orchestra at the Savoy Ballroom in Chicago.

Friday 19 November 1937

Ella Fitzgerald and the Chick Webb Orchestra close at the Palace Theatre in Chicago.

Ella Fitzgerald and the Chick Webb Orchestra play one-nighters in Dayton, Ohio, Knoxville, Tennessee and Cincinnati, Ohio before opening at the Palace Theatre in Cleveland, Ohio.

Thursday 25 November 1937

Ella Fitzgerald and the Chick Webb Orchestra open a one-week engagement at the Palace Theatre in Cleveland, Ohio.

December: Chick Webb Orchestra broadcasting via NBC's WEAF Red network Wednesdays (Thurs) 12:30am–1:00am, Thursdays 6:00pm–6:30pm and Fridays 12:00–12:30pm.

Wednesday 1 December 1937
Ella Fitzgerald and the Chick Webb Orchestra close at the Palace Theatre in Cleveland, Ohio.

Friday 3 December 1937
Ella Fitzgerald and the Chick Webb Orchestra play a one-nighter at the Savoy Theatre in Pittsburgh, Pa.

Saturday 4 December 1937
Ella Fitzgerald and the Chick Webb Orchestra play a one-nighter opposite the Wingy Manone Band at the Laurel Gardens in Newark, New Jersey.

Sunday 5 December 1937
Ella Fitzgerald and the Chick Webb Orchestra return to their residency at the Savoy Ballroom in New York City.

Friday 10 December 1937
Ella Fitzgerald and the Chick Webb Orchestra broadcast over WEAF from the Savoy Ballroom in New York City.
I Found A New Baby / After You (vEF) / *Bronzeville Stomp / She's Tall, She's Tan, She's Terrific* (vEF) / *Naughty Waltz / In A Little Spanish Town / You Showed Me The Way* (vEF) / *Royal Garden Blues / Honeysuckle Rose* (vEF)

Wednesday 15 December 1937
Ella Fitzgerald and the Chick Webb Orchestra broadcast over WEAF from the Savoy Ballroom in New York City.
After You've Gone / Love Is The Thing So They Say (vEF) / *My Blue Heaven / Love Is In My Heart / Don't Be That Way / Quaker City Jazz / Rock It For Me* (vEF) / *Naughty Waltz*

Thursday 16 December 1937
Ella Fitzgerald and the Chick Webb Orchestra broadcast from the Savoy Ballroom in New York City.
King Porter Stomp / Once In A While (vEF) / *Alabamy Stomp / Stop, Look And Listen / So Rare* (vEF) / *I've Got Rhythm*

Friday 17 December 1937
Ella Fitzgerald records with the Chick Webb Orchestra for Decca in New York City.
I Want To Be Happy (vEF, 2 takes) / *The Dipsy Doodle* (vEF) / *If Dreams Come True* (vEF) / *Hallelujah!* (vEF)
The band also records an instrumental: *Midnite In A Madhouse*

Later, Ella Fitzgerald and the Chick Webb Orchestra appear at a Monster Benefit Midnight Show at the Apollo Theatre in New York City. Other stars appearing include Bill Robinson, Cab Calloway, Rudy Vallee and Noble Sissle.

Sunday 19 December 1937
Ella Fitzgerald has a heavy cold and is unable to sing. Chick Webb arrives late at the Savoy Ballroom and only plays half the evening.

Monday 20 December 1937
Ella Fitzgerald and the Chick Webb Orchestra broadcast from the Savoy Ballroom in New York City.
My Blue Heaven / Once In A While (vEF) / *What A Shuffle / I'll Come To The Point* (vEF) / *Midnight In A Madhouse / Tall, Dark And Handsome / Rhythm In My Soul / I Want To Be Happy*

Tuesday 21 December 1937
Ella Fitzgerald and her Savoy Eight again record for Decca in New York City.
ELLA FITZGERALD (vocal), TAFT JORDAN (trumpet), SANDY WILLIAMS (trombone), LOUIS JORDAN (alto sax), TEDDY MCRAE (tenor sax/baritone sax), TOMMY FULFORD (piano), BOBBY JOHNSON (guitar), BEVERLY PEER (bass), CHICK WEBB (drums)
Bei Mir Bist Du Schoen (vEF) / *It's My Turn Now* (vEF)
Later, Ella Fitzgerald and the Chick Webb Orchestra broadcast from the Savoy Ballroom in New York City.
Clap Hands! Here Comes Charlie / True Confession (vEF) / *Sugar Foot Stomp / If Dreams Come True / Dipsy Doodle* (vEF) / *Bronzeville Stomp / Bei Mir Bist Du Schoen* (vEF) / *Royal Garden Blues*

Wednesday 22 December 1937
Ella Fitzgerald and the Chick Webb Orchestra close at the Savoy Ballroom to undertake another tour.

Friday 24 December 1937
Ella Fitzgerald and the Chick Webb Orchestra play a lunchtime concert at Osters Academy in Cleveland, Ohio. In the evening they play a dance at East Market Gardens in Akron, Ohio.

1938

Friday 1 January 1938

Ella Fitzgerald and the Chick Webb Orchestra play a New Year's Night Dance (10.00pm until 2.00am) at the Armory in Charleston, West Virginia.

Friday 7 January 1938

Ella Fitzgerald and the Chick Webb Orchestra open a one-week engagement at the Apollo Theatre in New York City. Also on the bill are Teddy Hale, Ventriloquist Holmes, Dippy, Dees & Dizzy, Four Box Brothers, Billy King, Swan & Lee and the 16 Harperettes.

Sunday 9 January 1938

Ella Fitzgerald and the Chick Webb Orchestra open a new season at the Savoy Ballroom in Harlem. For the first week they double at the Apollo Theatre.

January 15: Chick Webb Orchestra return to the air waves on Wednesdays 12:30am (NBC Blue network), Thursdays at 6:00pm and Fridays at midnight for NBC's Red network.

Wednesday 12 January 1938

Ella Fitzgerald and the Chick Webb Orchestra broadcast over WMCA (11.32pm until midnight) from the Apollo Theatre in New York City.
Midnight In A Madhouse / True Confession (vEF)

Thursday 13 January 1938

Ella Fitzgerald and the Chick Webb Orchestra close at the Apollo Theatre in New York City.

Sunday 16 January 1938

Ella Fitzgerald and the Chick Webb Orchestra appear in a Battle of Swing with Count Basie's Orchestra at the Savoy Ballroom in New York City.
Down Beat described the event:

The affair drew a record attendance and hundreds were turned away at the box office with the crowd tying up traffic for several blocks in that vicinity. Applause for both bands was tremendous and it was difficult to determine which band was the more popular.

Nevertheless, the ballot taken showed Chick Webb's band well in the lead over Basie's and Ella Fitzgerald well out in front over Billie Holliday [sic] and James Rushing…

Feeling ran very high between the supporters of the two bands, and it was a fight to the finish. Both bands played magnificently, with Basie having a particular appeal for the dancers, and Webb consistently stealing the show on the drums. Ella caused a sensation with her rendition of 'Loch Lomond', and Billie Holiday thrilled her fans with 'My Man'. When Ella sang she had the whole crowd rocking with her. James Rushing had everybody shouting the blues right along with him. Handkerchiefs were waving, people were shouting, the excitement was intense…

Thursday 20 January 1938

Ella Fitzgerald and the Chick Webb Orchestra broadcast over WNEW (12 to 12:30am) from the Savoy Ballroom.
If You Ever Should Leave (vEF) / *Quaker City Jazz* / *The Dipsy Doodle* (vEF) / *Go Harlem* / *True Confession* (vEF) / *I Found A New Baby*

Tuesday 25 January 1938
Ella Fitzgerald and her Savoy Eight record for Decca in New York City.
ELLA FITZGERALD (vocal), TAFT JORDAN (trumpet), SANDY WILLIAMS (trombone), LOUIS JORDAN (alto sax), TEDDY MCRAE (tenor sax/baritone sax), TOMMY FULFORD (piano), BOBBY JOHNSON (guitar), BEVERLY PEER (bass), CHICK WEBB (drums)
It's Wonderful (vEF) / *I Was Doing All Right* (vEF)

Wednesday 26 January 1938
Ella Fitzgerald and the Chick Webb Orchestra broadcast over WJZ (12:30 to 1:00am) from the Savoy Ballroom.
Tea For Two / Heart Of Mine (vEF) / *Somebody Loves Me / Naughty Waltz / You Took The Words Right Out Of My Heart / Clap Hands, Here Comes Charlie / It's Wonderful* (vEF) / *Copenhagen / King Porter Stomp*

Friday 28 January 1938
Ella Fitzgerald and the Chick Webb Orchestra open a one-week engagement at the Howard Theatre, Washington, D.C.

Thursday 3 February 1938
Ella Fitzgerald and the Chick Webb Orchestra close at the Howard Theatre in Washington, D.C.

Friday 4 February 1938
Ella Fitzgerald and the Chick Webb Orchestra play a one-nighter at the Strand Theatre in Baltimore, Maryland.

Monday 7 February 1938
Ella Fitzgerald and the Chick Webb Orchestra open a long engagement at the Flamingo Room of Levaggi's Restaurant in Boston. They are the first black band to play this spot. Sundays are off-nights.

Boston—During the bands stay here it can be heard via a coast-to-coast hook up over NBC's Blue network Tuesdays and Wednesdays at 12 midnight and Saturdays at 6:35pm.

Tuesday 14 February 1938
Ella Fitzgerald and the Chick Webb Orchestra broadcast (12 to 12:30am) from Levaggi's in Boston.
Blue Room / I Simply Adore You (vEF) / *D-Natural Blues / You're A Sweetheart* (vEF) / *If Dreams Come True* (vEF) / *Harlem Congo*

Thursday 3 March 1938
Ella Fitzgerald and the Chick Webb Orchestra broadcast (11:30pm to 12:00) from Levaggi's in Boston.
What A Shuffle / I Fall In Love With You Every Day (vEF) / *Blue Room / Midnight In A Madhouse / I'm Glad For Your Sake* (vEF) / *Tea For Two / I Simply Adore You* (vEF) / *Alabamy Home / Hallelujah*

CHICK WEBB HELD OVER IN BOSTON UNTIL MAY
NEW YORK CITY Mar.3—With his heart set on playing the almost color restricted Hippodrome Theatre in Baltimore, his home town, Chick Webb and his Savoy Swing Orchestra with vocalist Ella Fitzgerald, will have to forget the idea for a while as the option has been taken up on their services and they will have to remain in the Flamingo Room of Levaggi's nitery in Boston until May.

Saturday 5 March 1938
Ella Fitzgerald and the Chick Webb Orchestra broadcast (6:35pm to 7:00pm) from Levaggi's in Boston.

Monday 7 March 1938
Ella Fitzgerald and the Chick Webb Orchestra broadcast (12:00 to 12:30am) from Levaggi's in Boston.
Royal Garden Blues / Sweet As A Song (vEF) / *King Porter Stomp / Strictly Jive / In The Shade Of The New Apple Tree* (vEF) / *Stompin' At The Savoy / I'm Glad For Your Sake* (vEF) / *That's A-Plenty*

Due to previous commitments, Ella and Chick are unable to play Levaggi's on 11 and 12 March. They are replaced by Teddy Hill's Orchestra, the Four Ink Spots and the Savoy Big Apple Dancers.

Levaggi's
MASS. AVE. AT NORWAY ST.
Due to previous commitment
CHICK WEBB
Offers his friends a rare and memorable treat in Cafe History
2 Nights Only
Fri. Mar. 11-Sat. Mar. 12
SAVOY BIG APPLE DANCERS
MGM & RKO ARTISTS
FOUR INK SPOTS
NBC Novelty Quartette
TEDDY HILL and his
NBC SWING ORCHESTRA
Chick Webb returns to
FLAMINGO ROOM
MON., MAR. 14

Friday 11 March 1938
Ella Fitzgerald and the Chick Webb Orchestra play a Fraternity Dance (3.00am until 7.00am) in St. Elmo Fraternity Hall at Yale University in New Haven, Connecticut.

Saturday 12 March 1938
Ella Fitzgerald and the Chick Webb Orchestra play a concert and fraternity dance in Alpha Sigma Fraternity Hall at Yale University in New Haven, Connecticut. Before the concert Chick Webb is presented with an honorary degree.

Monday 14 March 1938
Ella Fitzgerald and the Chick Webb Orchestra return to the Flamingo Room of Levaggi's Restaurant in Boston.

Saturday 19 March 1938

Ella Fitzgerald and the Chick Webb Orchestra broadcast (6:35pm to 7:00pm) from Levaggi's in Boston.

Saturday 26 March 1938

Ella Fitzgerald and the Chick Webb Orchestra broadcast (6:35pm to 7:00pm) from Levaggi's in Boston.

Thursday 31 March 1938

Chick Webb is admitted to the Hudson View Hospital in New York to undergo surgery. Chick's friend, Scrippy, takes over on drums for the two weeks that Webb is absent.

Saturday 2 April 1938

Ella Fitzgerald and the Chick Webb Orchestra broadcast (6:35pm to 7:00pm) from Levaggi's in Boston.

Saturday 9 April 1938

Ella Fitzgerald and the Chick Webb Orchestra broadcast (6:35pm to 7:00pm) from Levaggi's in Boston.

Sunday 10 April 1938

Ella Fitzgerald is a guest artist, and one of the judges for Martin Block's Swing Contest, at the Savoy Ballroom.

Saturday 16 April 1938

Ella Fitzgerald and the Chick Webb Orchestra broadcast (6:35pm to 7:00pm) from Levaggi's in Boston.

Thursday 21 April 1938

Chick Webb takes time off from Levaggi's to fly down to New York to take part in an invited jam session (7.30–9.30pm) with the Tommy Dorsey Orchestra at the Paramount Theatre. Also taking part are Duke Ellington, Jack Teagarden and Kay Thompson. Paramount booking agent Harry Kalcheim is reportedly so impressed with Chick's drumming that he strongly considers a Paramount booking for the Webb band.

Saturday 23 April 1938

Ella Fitzgerald and the Chick Webb Orchestra broadcast (6:35pm to 7:00pm) from Levaggi's in Boston.

Monday 25 April 1938

Ella Fitzgerald's 20th birthday.

Saturday 30 April 1938

Ella Fitzgerald and the Chick Webb Orchestra broadcast (6:35pm to 7:00pm) from Levaggi's in Boston.
During the long engagement at Levaggi's Ella has been working on revamping an old nursey rhyme. She takes it to Van Alexander who arranges it for the band and *A-Tisket, A-Tasket* is born.

Monday 2 May 1938

Ella Fitzgerald records with the Chick Webb Orchestra for Decca in New York City.
ELLA FITZGERALD (vocal), MARIO BAUZA, TAFT JORDAN, BOBBY STARK (trumpets), SANDY WILLIAMS, NAT STORY, GEORGE MATTHEWS (trombones), LOUIS JORDAN (alto sax), GARVIN BUSHELL (clarinet/alto sax), TEDDY McRAE (tenor sax), WAYMAN CARVER (tenor sax/flute), TOMMY FULFORD (piano), BOBBY JOHNSON (guitar), BEVERLY PEER (bass), CHICK WEBB (drums)
A-Tisket, A-Tasket (vEF) / *Heart Of Mine* (vEF) / *I'm Just A Jitterbug* (vEF)
The band also records an instrumental: *Azure*

Tuesday 3 May 1938

Ella Fitzgerald and her Savoy Eight record for Decca in New York City.
ELLA FITZGERALD (vocal), TAFT JORDAN (trumpet), SANDY WILLIAMS (trombone), LOUIS JORDAN (alto sax), TEDDY McRAE (tenor sax/baritone sax), TOMMY FULFORD (piano), BOBBY JOHNSON (guitar), BEVERLY PEER (bass), CHICK WEBB (drums)
This Time It's Real / What Do You Know About Love? / You Can't Be Mine / We Can't Go On This Way / Saving Myself For You / If YouOnly Knew
The full band also records two instrumentals: *Spinnin' The Webb / Liza*

Wednesday 4 May 1938

Ella Fitzgerald and the Chick Webb Orchestra close at the Flamingo Room of Levaggi's Restaurant in Boston.

Alto saxist Louis Jordan (*left*) attempts to recruit Ella and other members of the orchestra for his new band. He has been having an affair with Ella, possibly a ruse on his part to entice her to join his new enterprise. Chick Webb is furious and fires Jordan. By the time they reach New York, Hilton Jefferson has replaced him.

Thursday 5 May 1938

Ella Fitzgerald and the Chick Webb Orchestra open a one-week engagement at the RKO Theatre in Boston. Also on the bill are Derby Wilson and Holmes & Henry. The movie presentation is 'Go Chase Yourself' starring Lucille Ball.

Wednesday 11 May 1938

Ella Fitzgerald and the Chick Webb Orchestra close at the RKO Theatre in Boston.

Wednesday 25 May 1938

Ella Fitzgerald and the Chick Webb Orchestra play a dance (9.00pm until 2.00am) at the Mercantile Hall in Philadelphia.

Friday 27 May 1938

Ella Fitzgerald and the Chick Webb Orchestra open a two-week engagement at the Apollo Theatre in New York City. Also on the bill are Nicodemus, Ventriloquist Holmes, Helena & Joe Smith, the Three Yams and the 16 Harperettes. Chick's is the first band to play successive weeks at the Apollo.

Sunday 29 May 1938

Ella Fitzgerald and the Chick Webb Orchestra play an outdoor benefit for Musicians Union Local 802 at the Randall's Island Stadium in New York City. The 'Carnival of Swing' (11am–4.45pm) organised by Martin Block features more than 20 bands and attracts a crowd of 25,000. Ella and the band are featured in a live broadcast from the stadium (11:00am to 12:30pm) over WNEW.

Below: Ella, Chick and the band are pictured during their live Sunday morning WNEW broadcast from the 'Carnival of Swing' at Randall's Island Stadium in New York City.

Thursday 9 June 1938

Ella Fitzgerald records with the Chick Webb Orchestra for Decca in New York City.

ELLA FITZGERALD (vocal), MARIO BAUZA, TAFT JORDAN, BOBBY STARK (trumpets), SANDY WILLIAMS, NAT STORY, GEORGE MATTHEWS (trombones), HILTON JEFFERSON (alto sax), GARVIN BUSHELL (clarinet/alto sax), TED MCRAE (tenor sax), WAYMAN CARVER (tenor sax/flute), TOMMY FULFORD (piano), BOBBY JOHNSON (guitar), BEVERLY PEER (bass), CHICK WEBB (drums)
Pack Up Your Sins (And Go To The Devil) (vEF) / *MacPherson Is Rehearsin'* (vEF) / *Everybody Step* (vEF) / *Ella* (vEF, TJ)

Ella Fitzgerald and the Chick Webb Orchestra close at the Apollo Theatre in New York City.

Friday 10 June 1938

Ella Fitzgerald and the Chick Webb Orchestra play a dance (8.30pm until 1.00am) at Canobie Lake Park in Salem, New Hampshire.

Saturday 11 June 1938

Ella Fitzgerald and the Chick Webb Orchestra play a dance at the Old Orchard Pier, Old Orchard Beach, Portland, Maine.

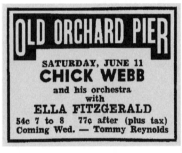

Sunday 12 June 1938

Ella Fitzgerald and the Chick Webb Orchestra play Lambda Delta's 15th Annual Dance (9.00pm until 2.00am) at Danceland in Rochester, New York.

Monday 13 June 1938

Ella Fitzgerald and the Chick Webb Orchestra play a dance at the Trianon Ballroom in Cleveland, Ohio.

Tuesday 14 June 1938

Ella Fitzgerald and the Chick Webb Orchestra play a Senior Prom Dance at Oberlin College Auditorium in Oberlin, Ohio.

Wednesday 15 June 1938

Ella Fitzgerald and the Chick Webb Orchestra arrive in Chicago and settle into the Grand Hotel.

Friday 17 June 1938

Ella Fitzgerald and the Chick Webb Orchestra open a one-week engagement at the Oriental Theatre in Chicago. The movie presentation is 'Crime School' starring Humphrey Bogart, Gale Page and The Dead End Kids.

Thursday 23 June 1938

Ella Fitzgerald and the Chick Webb Orchestra close at the Oriental Theatre in Chicago.

Friday 24 June 1938

Ella Fitzgerald and the Chick Webb Orchestra open a one-week engagement at the Fox Theatre in Detroit, Michigan. Also on the bill are The Nicholas Brothers and a huge Harlem revue.

Thursday 30 June 1938

Ella Fitzgerald and the Chick Webb Orchestra close at the Fox Theatre in Detroit, Michigan.

Friday 1 July 1938

Ella Fitzgerald and the Chick Webb Orchestra play a one-nighter at the Brant Inn Sky Club in Burlington, Ontario, Canada.

Tuesday 5 July 1938

Ella Fitzgerald and the Chick Webb Orchestra play a one-nighter at Hillside View in Bluefield, West Virginia.

Wednesday 6 July 1938
Ella Fitzgerald and the Chick Webb Orchestra play a one-nighter at Mt. Hope Armory in Beckley, West Virginia.

Saturday 9 July 1938
Ella Fitzgerald and the Chick Webb Orchestra play a one-nighter at the Conneaut Beach Pier at Conneaut Lake, Pennsylvania.

Monday 11 July 1938
Ella Fitzgerald and the Chick Webb Orchestra play a dance at the Graystone Ballroom in Detroit, Michigan.

Friday 15 July 1938
Ella Fitzgerald and the Chick Webb Orchestra play a dance (9.00pm until 2.00am) at the Memorial Hall in Dayton, Ohio.

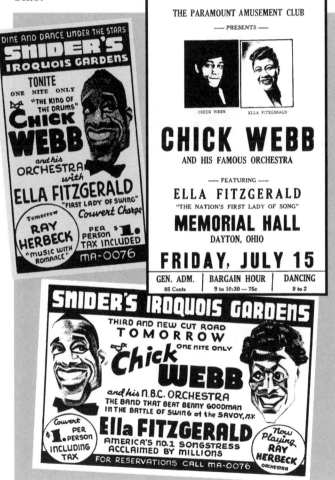

Wednesday 20 July 1938
Ella Fitzgerald and the Chick Webb Orchestra play a one-nighter at Snider's Iroquois Gardens in Louisville, Kentucky.

Friday 22 July 1938
Ella Fitzgerald and the Chick Webb Orchestra play a one-nighter at the Coliseum in St. Louis, Missouri.

Saturday 23 July 1938
Ella Fitzgerald and the Chick Webb Orchestra play a dance (8.00pm until 1.00am) at Forest Park Highlands in St. Louis, Missouri.

Sunday 24 July 1938
Ella Fitzgerald and the Chick Webb Orchestra play a dance at Fairyland Park in Kansas City, Missouri.

Monday 25 July 1938
Ella Fitzgerald and the Chick Webb Orchestra play a concert at the Municipal Auditorium in Kansas City, Missouri.

Sunday 31 July 1938
Ella Fitzgerald and the Chick Webb Orchestra a Battle of Bands with the Horace Henderson Orchestra at the Savoy Ballroom in Chicago. An estimated crowd of 6,000 attend.

Wednesday 3 August 1938
Ella Fitzgerald and the Chick Webb Orchestra play a dance at the Waco Ballroom in Syracuse, New York.

Thursday 4 August 1938
Ella Fitzgerald and the Chick Webb Orchestra play a dance at Tomlinson Hall in Indianapolis, Indiana.

Wednesday 10 August 1938

Ella Fitzgerald and the Chick Webb Orchestra open a one-week engagement at the Paramount Theatre in New York City. Also on the bill are Chuck & Chuckles, The Charioteers and the Savoy Lindy Hoppers. The movie presentation is 'Give Me A Sailor' starring Martha Raye and Bob Hope.

Right: Ella and Chick on stage at the Paramount Theatre in Times Square while (below) their names light up the Broadway scene.

Saturday 13 August 1938
Ella Fitzgerald and the Chick Webb Orchestra appear on WNEW's 'Saturday Night Swing Club' at the NBC Studios in New York City.
I've Been Saving Myself For You

Chick Webb and Ella Fitzgerald did an "Eyston" recently when they went off the air at 8.15, had a speed elevator waiting for them, a fast cab to whirl them through thirteen blocks of heavy traffic, and be on the Paramount, New York, stage by 8.20. And they did it! Good thing Chick has two sets of drums.

Tuesday 16 August 1938
Ella Fitzgerald and the Chick Webb Orchestra close at the Paramount Theatre in New York City.

Wednesday 17 August 1938
Ella Fitzgerald records with the Chick Webb Orchestra for Decca in New York City.
ELLA FITZGERALD (vocal), MARIO BAUZA, TAFT JORDAN, BOBBY STARK (trumpets), SANDY WILLIAMS, NAT STORY,GEORGE MATTHEWS (trombones), HILTON JEFFERSON (alto sax), GARVIN BUSHELL (clarinet/alto sax), TED McRAE (tenor sax), WAYMAN CARVER (tenor sax/flute), TOMMY FULFORD (piano), BOBBY JOHNSON (guitar), BEVERLY PEER (bass), CHICK WEBB (drums)
Wacky Dust (vEF) / *Gotta Pebble In My Shoe* (vEF) / *I Can't Stop Loving You* (vEF) / *Ella* (vEF, TJ)

Thursday 18 August 1938
Ella Fitzgerald records with the Chick Webb Orchestra for Decca in New York City.
ELLA FITZGERALD (vocal), MARIO BAUZA, TAFT JORDAN, BOBBY STARK (trumpets), SANDY WILLIAMS, NAT STORY, GEORGE MATTHEWS (trombones), HILTON JEFFERSON (alto sax), GARVIN BUSHELL (clarinet/alto sax), TED McRAE (tenor sax), WAYMAN CARVER (tenor sax/flute), TOMMY FULFORD (piano), BOBBY JOHNSON (guitar), BEVERLY PEER (bass), CHICK WEBB (drums)
I Let A Tear Fall In The River (vEF)
The band records an instrumental, *Who Ya Hunchin'?*, and Ella records with her Savoy Eight at the same session.
ELLA FITZGERALD (vocal), TAFT JORDAN (trumpet), SANDY WILLIAMS (trombone), HILTON JEFFERSON (alto sax), TEDDY McRAE (tenor sax/baritone sax), TOMMY FULFORD (piano), BOBBY JOHNSON (guitar), BEVERLY PEER (bass), CHICK WEBB (drums)
Strictly From Dixie / *Woe Is Me*

Friday 19 August 1938
Ella Fitzgerald and the Chick Webb Orchestra play a one-nighter at the Bal-a-l'air in Worcester, Massachusetts.

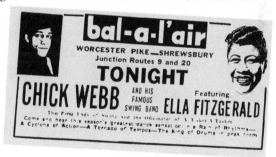

Saturday 3 September 1938
Ella Fitzgerald and the Chick Webb Orchestra play a dance at the Casino Ballroom in Asbury Park, New Jersey.

Socko Chick

Heavy Money Basket

ASBURY PARK, N.J. — Chick Webb and Ella Fitzgerald proved to be a socko attraction on Saturday, when they played here for Walter Reed at the Boardwalk Casino.
The combination equalled the attendance mark of Horace Heidt, set last year in bringing out 3,700 persons.
Webb had 1,200 spectators jamming the balcony at two-bits a seat, and over 2,500 dancers on the floor at eighty-five cents each, hitting a heavy money basket of over $2,500, which has been topped by Sammy Kaye only, whose take on July 4 was $4,500.

Sunday 4 September 1938
Ella Fitzgerald and the Chick Webb Orchestra play a dance (12 midnight until 4.00am) at the City Auditorium in Atlanta, Georgia.

Monday 5 September 1938

Ella Fitzgerald and the Chick Webb Orchestra play a one-nighter at the Macon Auditorium in Macon, Georgia.

It seems likely that they continue south for a tour of Florida, taking in Miami, Tampa, Jacksonville and Madison before returning north.

LABOR DAY SPECIAL
J. Neal Montgomery
Presents
CHICK WEBB
"The King of the Drums"
And His Orchestra
FEATURING:
Ella Fitzgerald
"The First Lady of Swing"
MACON AUDITORIUM
Tomorrow night at 8:30 o'clock. Reserved section for white patrons Tickets on sale Mitchell, Williams and Mack Admission. Advance Tickets 55c. Tickets at Door 65c.

Swing Exponents Make Jitterbugs of Maconites

Negroes Dance and Whites Listen to Music of Webb and Fitzgerald

By JAMES C. BURKE

Fifteen cats rocked with reckless abandon at the Macon auditorium last night, turning several thousand white and Negro swing fans into jitterbugs of the first order.

Playing in their celebrated strong-beat rhythm, Chick Webb and his 15-piece dance band set a blood-tingling pace for local jive addicts, but dusky singer Ella Fitzgerald held the evening's spotlight.

Ella, nationally famous for her rendition of A Tisket A Tasket, a composition she wrote several months ago, was encored again and again by the audience, frenzied from her spirited expression.

"I picked out the melody from the drop-the-handkerchief game I used to play at school," Ella explained backstage, "and when I told Chick about it he suggested we record it and it might go over."

The song version, in which a "lost little yellow basket" is substituted for the dropped handkerchief, took the country by storm before the first wax impression had time to cool. Though it has been copied by various bands and singers, Ella's style is still acclaimed "tops."

Ella's Just 20

The young Negress, who has just passed her 20th birthday, was born in Yonkers, N. Y., and was "discovered" by Webb at an amateur contest in New York City four years ago.

"She's without a doubt the best attraction I've got since she started A Tisket," remarked Webb, a diminutive Negro whom many recognize as one of the best drummers in the profession. "On the present Southern tour, she's been asked to repeat that song at least seven or eight times a night."

The swing-songstress, comely and buxom, is a bundle of energy, lifting her skirts and trucking while performing before the "mike." Even in her seat she is forced to move in time with the wildish tones sent out by the 15 "chicks."

"I'm crazy about dancing," she confessed, "and do the shag and lindy-hop whenever I get a chance."

The band leader is a native New Yorker and boasts convincingly that "Gotham is the greatest city in the world."

"New York Stamp"

"Everything and everybody gets started there," Chick claimed. "You haven't seen a successful movie star or street sweeper who didn't begin there. You've got to have the New York stamp on you before you get anywhere."

While more than 500 white enthusiasts looked on from balcony sections, Negro couples in gay evening wear danced on the floor below.

A few young Negroes gathered in various corners, and even behind the stage, pounding out rhythm with as many capers as their ingenuity would permit.

"I ain't been dancing but three years," offered Clarence Abrams, small 13-year-older in shorts and tennis shoes from 123 Williams Lane, "but I can swing."

Sunday 18 September 1938

Ella Fitzgerald and the Chick Webb Orchestra open a one-week engagement at the State Theatre in Hartford, Connecticut.

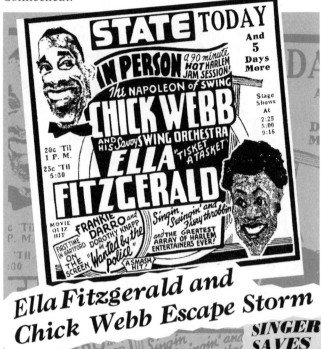

Ella Fitzgerald and Chick Webb Escape Storm

Tuesday 20 September 1938

Hartford and other New England cities suffer tremendous damage when a hurricane hits inland areas on Tuesday evening. Shortly after Ella, Chick and the band have left, the theatre roof is blown off, forcing the immediate closure.

Tuesday 27 September 1938

Ella Fitzgerald and the Chick Webb Orchestra play a dance at the Butterfly Ballroom in Springfield, Massachusetts.

Thursday 6 October 1938

Ella Fitzgerald records with the Chick Webb Orchestra for Decca in New York City.

ELLA FITZGERALD (vocal), DICK VANCE, TAFT JORDAN, BOBBY STARK (trumpets), SANDY WILLIAMS, NAT STORY, GEORGE MATTHEWS (trombones), HILTON JEFFERSON (alto sax), GARVIN BUSHELL (clarinet/alto sax), TED MCRAE (tenor sax), WAYMAN CARVER (tenor sax/flute), TOMMY FULFORD (piano), BOBBY JOHNSON (guitar), BEVERLY PEER (bass), CHICK WEBB (drums)

F.D.R. Jones (vEF) / *I Love Each Move You Make* (vEF) / *It's Foxy* (vEF) / *I Found My Yellow Basket* (vEF)

SINGER SAVES PUPPY

HARTFORD, Conn. — Chick Webb and his band, and Ella Fitzgerald, vocalist, narrowly escaped death here last week when the worst storm ever seen in Northeastern America struck the State Theatre here where they were playing an engagement.

A few minutes after the members of the band and Miss Fitzgerald had vacated the theatre, the roof was blown off. Several workmen who were in the building packing up the effects of the Chick Webb troup miraculously escaped injury.

An hour later, the overflowing river had flooded the theatre, up to the second floor.

Saw Dog

As the Chick Webb band was leaving the theatre, Ella saw a small dog struggling in the water. She leaped into the swirling flood, despite the cries of orchestra men for her to come back.

But Ella did not stop until she had the small dog in her arms, and she and the puppy, both wet to the skin, and cold and shivering, were hauled back into the boat.

While the storm was at its height, Chick stood at the top of a building, gazing at the swirling water, the thousands of homeless persons, and the general havoc done by the storm.

He took a sheet of paper and began to jot down a few notes, and the result is a new song, "I Let a Tear Fall into the River," which is to be published soon.

Friday 7 October 1938

Ella Fitzgerald and the Chick Webb Orchestra open a one-week engagement at the Earle Theatre in Philadelphia.

Thursday 13 October 1938

Ella Fitzgerald and the Chick Webb Orchestra close at the Earle Theatre in Philadelphia.

Friday 14 October 1938

Ella Fitzgerald and the Chick Webb Orchestra open a one-week engagement at the Stanley Theatre in Pittsburgh, Pennsylvania.

Thursday 20 October 1938

Ella Fitzgerald and the Chick Webb Orchestra close at the Stanley Theatre in Pittsburgh, Pennsylvania.

Friday 21 October 1938

Ella Fitzgerald and the Chick Webb Orchestra open a one-week engagement at the Hippodrome Theatre in Baltimore, Maryland. Also on the bill are Chuck & Chuckles and the Six Lindy Hoppers.

Sunday 23 October 1938

Ella Fitzgerald and the Chick Webb Orchestra play an afternoon engagement in Camden, New Jersey.

Wednesday 26 October 1938

Ella Fitzgerald and the Chick Webb Orchestra play a midnight benefit at the Royal Theatre after their stint at the Hippodrome in Baltimore, Maryland.

Thursday 27 October 1938

Ella Fitzgerald and the Chick Webb Orchestra close at the Hippodrome Theatre in Baltimore, Maryland.

Wednesday 2 November 1938

Ella Fitzgerald and the Chick Webb Orchestra play a dance at the Trianon Ballroom in Cleveland, Ohio.

Variety is at the Hippodrome opening and reports on an ovation for Ella and big business at the box-office.

HIPP, BALTO

Baltimore, Oct. 22.
Chick Webb Orch, Ella Fitzgerald, Chuck & Chuckles, Lindy Hoppers (4); 'Girls' School' (Col)

First hometown appearance of Chick Webb since hitting the upper brackets is a killer-diller—and how! Walloping out 45 minutes of solid swing, Webb, Fitzgerald, etc., are not only attracting the town's cats and sending in robust style, but drawing many conservative, curious stub-holders.

With Webb modestly seated behind his drums band is fronted by personable stick-weaver from the band, who pleasingly handles the layout. Opening number by band, however, quickly reveals prowess of Webb at the hides and he gets show off to a rousing start. Pace holds with appearance of four Lindy Hoppers next, who set right spot for band's jam session which follows.

'King Porter Stomp, by band, with solo members going to town and audience joining hand-clapping, holds hectic pace and precedes Chuck and Chuckles, whose hotcha legmania ties up matters tightly. They're difficult to follow, but Ella Fitzgerald does that to an ovation. Sings 'You Go to My Head,' 'Jitterbug,' 'Saving Myself for You and the inevitable 'A-Tisket.' Entire ensemble joins in lengthy, but effective, swing finale.

Biz big.   *Burm.*

Friday 4 November 1938
Ella Fitzgerald and the Chick Webb Orchestra open a one-week engagement at Shea's Buffalo Theatre in Buffalo, New York. Also on the bill are Stump & Stumpy. The movie presentation is 'Listen, Darling' starring Judy Garland and Freddie Bartholomew.

Thursday 10 November 1938
Ella Fitzgerald and the Chick Webb Orchestra close at Shea's Buffalo Theatre in Buffalo, New York.

Friday 11 November 1938
Ella Fitzgerald and the Chick Webb Orchestra open a one-week engagement at the Rivoli Theatre in Toledo, Ohio.

Thursday 17 November 1938
Ella Fitzgerald and the Chick Webb Orchestra close at the Rivoli Theatre in Toledo, Ohio.

Friday 18 November 1938
Ella Fitzgerald and the Chick Webb Orchestra open a one-week engagement at the Regal Theatre in Chicago. The movie presentation is 'Sing You Sinners' starring Bing Crosby.

Thursday 24 November 1938
Ella Fitzgerald and the Chick Webb Orchestra close at the Regal Theatre in Chicago.

Sunday 27 November 1938
Ella Fitzgerald and the Chick Webb Orchestra play a dance at the Casa Loma Ballroom in St. Louis, Missouri.

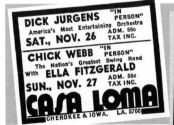

Monday 28 November 1938
Ella Fitzgerald and the Chick Webb Orchestra play a dance at the Coliseum in St. Louis, Missouri.

Thursday 1 December 1938
Ella Fitzgerald and the Chick Webb Orchestra open a one-week engagement at the Newman Theatre in Kansas City, Kansas. The movie presentation is 'Thanks For The Memory' starring Bob Hope and Shirley Ross.

Tuesday 6 December 1938
Tuesday night is request night at the Newman Theatre.

Right:
Variety *reviews the show at the Newman Theatre.*

NEWMAN, K. C.

Kansas City, Dec. 2.
Chick Webb orchestra (13), Ella Fitzgerald, Stump & Stumpy, Lindy Hoppers (4); 'Thanks for the Memory' (Par).

This house, operated by Paramount, largely on films only, has pinned some hopes on flesh as a means of combating the usual pre-holiday doldrums at the b.o., and the first assignment is given to Webb.

Theme of the show is swing tunes, catering to the bugs and jivers throughout. It's hot music from start to finish of the well-trimmed 45 minutes.

Opening is carried by the band, following introduction of the leader, giving a fit sample of what's to follow. Two couples of Lindy hoppers come in fast pace, with band and m.c. joining in the spirit of rhythm.

Quintette of piano, flute, clarinet, doghouse and Webb on the drums is featured with a torrid but classy 'Stomping at the Savoy' and 'One O'Clock Jump.' Group is easily a mainstay of the band.

Stump and Stumpy bring on their dancing, patter, imitations and general clowning. Team shows to best advantage in their stepping, clowning being overdone and somewhat blank for lack of material.

Remainder of time is given over to Ella Fitzgerald, who shares billing with Webb. She includes 'My Reverie,' which is not quite her type, but capably done; 'I'm a Jitterbug' and 'Tisket.' She leads into 'St. Louis Blues,' which winds the show with all hands taking part in the final jam session.

Biz okay as town has more than its share of jitterbugs.   *Quin.*

Wednesday 7 December 1938
Ella Fitzgerald and the Chick Webb Orchestra close at the Newman Theatre in Kansas City, Kansas.

Thursday 8 December 1938
Ella Fitzgerald and the Chick Webb Orchestra play a dance (9.00pm until 1.00am) for the Jane Phillips Sorority at the JPS Clubhouse in Bartlesville, Oklahoma. The dance is broadcast(10:15 to 10:30pm and 11:15 to11:30pm) over station KVOO in Tulsa.

Friday 9 December 1938
Ella Fitzgerald and the Chick Webb Orchestra play a one-nighter at the Tulsa Coliseum in Tulsa, Oklahoma.

Saturday 10 December 1938
Ella Fitzgerald and the Chick Webb Orchestra play a dance (9.30pm until 3.00am) at Blossom Heath in Oklahoma City, Oklahoma.

Sunday 11 December 1938
Ella Fitzgerald and the Chick Webb Orchestra play a dance at the Fair Park Roller Rink in Dallas, Texas.

Ella Fitzgerald and the Chick Webb Orchestra play a dance in Galveston, Texas. The promoters, Earl Cawthorne and George Whiteside run off with the proceeds but are caught and arrested.

Saturday 17 December 1938
Ella Fitzgerald and the Chick Webb Orchestra play a one-nighter at the Blue Moon Club in Bunkie, Louisiana.

Monday 26 December 1938
Ella Fitzgerald and the Chick Webb Orchestra play a dance (9.00pm until 2.00am) at the Fleischer Auditorium of the YMCA in Philadelphia.

Tuesday 27 December 1938
Ella Fitzgerald and the Chick Webb Orchestra play a one-nighter at the Essex Country Club in West Orange, New Jersey.

Monday 2 January 1939
Ella Fitzgerald and the Chick Webb Orchestra open a 5-day engagement at the State Theatre, Hartford, Connecticut. Also on the bill are Slim & Slam and Stump & Stumpy.

Friday 6 January 1939
Ella Fitzgerald and the Chick Webb Orchestra close at the State Theatre, Hartford, Connecticut.

Monday 9 January 1939
The Chick Webb Orchestra are recorded by RCA Victor for NBC Transcription in New York City, but Ella does not feature.

Friday 13 January 1939
Ella Fitzgerald and the Chick Webb Orchestra open a one-week engagement at the Apollo Theatre in New York City. Also on the bill are Norman & Blake, Bobbie & Teddy Drinkard, Four Swingsters & Edith King, Jackie 'Moms' Mabley and Johnnie LaRue.

Sunday 15 January 1939
Ella Fitzgerald and the Chick Webb Orchestra play a Benefit for Underprivileged Children at the Renaissance Casino in New York City.

APOLLO, N. Y.

Chick Webb Orch (14) Ella Fitzgerald, Jackie Mabley, John LaRue, Norman & Blake, Swingsters (3), Edith King, Vivian Harris, The Drinkhards; 'Sharpshooters' (20th).

There's Harlemania aplenty here this week in the persons of Chick Webb's orchestra and Ella Fitzgerald, who're somewhat of an anomaly in this spot. Further downtown at the Paramount, where these two played, they beat the customers down to their socks in short order; at this Harlem house, where there usually can't be enough swing to satiate the payees, it was a bit different opening night. It was somewhat of a decorous crowd that viewed the show.

It's all Webb and Fitzgerald here and the customers' appreciation of their efforts is made manifold because of the extreme disparity with the rest of the bill, which is only mediocre.

Webb remains at the drums and has a young band-member fronting for him, but the spotlight is continually on Webb. His expert tattoo on the skins is evident throughout, though his mannerisms are more subdued than the average drummer. Rest of the band is excellent, though also marked by the subdued mannerisms of their leader.

Band starts off with 'Harlem Stride,' which is a mild opener, but then hits the groove with 'Stompin' at the Savoy. 'Liza' hits the top note with the customers, and not unduly, since the crew does that best. It's a Webb recording for Decca.

Miss Fitzgerald is plenty solid with her tunes, swing and sweet alike. First impression of her is that she's the conservative type, particularly in 'Heart and Soul,' which she does plaintively and well. But 'FDR Jones' completely dispels that. Latter is done expertly, but by no means approaches the click results usually gained in ensembling the number, which made the tune go over so mightily in the 'Sing Out the News' revue. As is, a couple of the musicians chorus occasionally, but that's not enough.

She's mixing 'em up cleverly, following with 'I Let a Tear Fall,' which is announced as written by Webb, and then comes through with 'St. Louis Blues,' which features a couple of the band members instrumentally. Tune that secured Miss Fitzgerald prominence, 'A-Tisket,' is properly ignored here, since it's stalemated by now, but she does a sequel to that, 'Found Yellow Basket,' which scores.

Eighty-minute show is opened by the house's usual sketches, which feature Jackie Mabley, John La Rue and Vivian Harris. Their usual blue stuff is tempered considerably this week. There's some aside instrumentaling by the Swingsters (3) that's good and Edith King does some mediocre singing. The Drinkhards are a fair mixed comedy dance team. Norman and Blake are male tapsters who work in cutaways and click. Their routines are off the beaten path. The house line is on in three spots, but was missing opening night.

Band is on stage during the earlier part of the show, accompanying behind a scrim, and when the latter lifts is revealed in a nifty setting. Rest of production, however, is off. Snowstorm exacted its toll at the xxoffice opening night (14).

Ella to Wed

New York—Ella Fitzgerald, plump chanteuse with Chick Webb, will go to the altar this month while the band is at the Park Central Hotel. Everything's all set except that Ella won't reveal the name of the groom. Webb has given his official okeh.

Thursday 19 January 1939
Ella Fitzgerald and the Chick Webb Orchestra close at the Apollo Theatre in New York City.

Saturday 21 January 1939
Ella Fitzgerald and the Chick Webb Orchestra broadcast on CBS' Saturday Night Swing Club at the NBC Studios in New York City.
I Let A Tear Fall In The River (vEF)

Wednesday 25 January 1939
Ella Fitzgerald and the Chick Webb Orchestra open a 4-week engagement at the Cocoanut Grove atop the Park Central Hotel in New York City. The Four Ink Spots and Derby Wilson are also on the bill. On opening night, Ella and Chick broadcast from the Cocoanut Grove (11:30pm to midnight) via WOR over the NBC network.

Thursday 26 January 1939
Ella Fitzgerald and the Chick Webb Orchestra broadcast from the Cocoanut Grove (11:30pm to midnight) via WJZ over the NBC network.

Right: Ella Fitzgerald sings for the dancers at the Cocoanut Grove while Bardu Ali conducts. Chick can be seen at the left.

Friday 27 January 1939
Ella Fitzgerald and the Chick Webb Orchestra broadcast from the Cocoanut Grove (12 to 12:30am) via WJZ over the NBC network.

Saturday 28 January 1939
Ella Fitzgerald and the Chick Webb Orchestra broadcast from the Cocoanut Grove (12 to 12:30am) via WJZ over the NBC network.

Wednesday 1 February 1939
Ella Fitzgerald and the Chick Webb Orchestra broadcast from the Cocoanut Grove (12 to 12:30am) via WJZ over the NBC network.

Friday 3 February 1939
Ella Fitzgerald and the Chick Webb Orchestra broadcast from the Cocoanut Grove (12 to 12:30am) via WJZ over the NBC network.

Saturday 4 February 1939
Ella Fitzgerald and the Chick Webb Orchestra broadcast from the Cocoanut Grove (12 to 12:30am) via WJZ over the NBC network.

Tuesday 7 February 1939
Ella Fitzgerald and the Chick Webb Orchestra broadcast from the Cocoanut Grove (11:30pm to midnight) via WOR over the NBC network.

Wednesday 8 February 1939
Ella Fitzgerald and the Chick Webb Orchestra broadcast from the Cocoanut Grove (12 to 12:30am) via WJZ over the NBC network.

Friday 10 February 1939
Ella Fitzgerald and the Chick Webb Orchestra broadcast from the Cocoanut Grove (12 to 12:30am) via WJZ over the NBC network.
Let's Get Together (theme) / *Blue Room* / *Deep In A Dream* (vEF) / *One O'Clock Jump* / *That Was My Heart* (vEF)

Saturday 11 February 1939
Ella Fitzgerald and the Chick Webb Orchestra broadcast from the Cocoanut Grove (12 to 12:30am) via WJZ over the NBC network.

Tuesday 14 February 1939
Ella Fitzgerald and the Chick Webb Orchestra broadcast from the Cocoanut Grove (11:30pm to midnight) via WOR over the NBC network.

Friday 17 February 1939
Ella Fitzgerald records with the Chick Webb Orchestra for Decca in New York City.
ELLA FITZGERALD (vocal), DICK VANCE, TAFT JORDAN, BOBBY STARK (trumpets), SANDY WILLIAMS, NAT STORY, GEORGE MATTHEWS (trombones), HILTON JEFFERSON (alto sax), GARVIN BUSHELL (clarinet/alto sax), TED McRAE (tenor sax), WAYMAN CARVER (tenor sax/flute), TOMMY FULFORD (piano), BOBBY JOHNSON (guitar), BEVERLY PEER (bass), CHICK WEBB (drums)
Undecided (vEF) / *'Tain't What You Do* (vEF) / *One Side Of Me* (vEF) / *My Heart Belongs To Daddy* (vEF)
The full band also records an instrumental: *In The Groove At The Grove*

Saturday 18 February 1939
Ella Fitzgerald and the Chick Webb Orchestra broadcast from the Cocoanut Grove (12 to 12:30am) via WJZ over the NBC network.

Tuesday 21 February 1939
Ella Fitzgerald and the Chick Webb Orchestra broadcast from the Cocoanut Grove (11:30pm to midnight) via WOR over the NBC network.

Wednesday 22 February 1939
Ella Fitzgerald and the Chick Webb Orchestra close at the Cocoanut Grove atop the Park Central Hotel in New York City.

COCOANUT GROVE
(PARK CENTRAL HOTEL, N. Y.)

Variety reviews the band at the Cocoanut Grove.

Chick Webb orch, Ella Fitzgerald, Bardou Ali, Four Inkspots, Derby Wilson.

Park Central follows the lead of other N. Y. hotels in switching from the softer, sweeter style of musical fare to jitterbug rhythms, and indications point to Chick Webb being a hypo for the Grove. His crew is popular in New York, and its scheduled five-weekly air shots will help its draw.

Only thing which can possibly stymie the success of the four-week date with options is the upped cover, which amounts to 75c. after 11 p.m. weekdays and $1.50 per on weekends. However, some of the other spots in town, catering to the younger trade, are getting that figure and claim to be doing okay.

Insertion of Webb in the Grove, a spot where softly lighted, serene surroundings seemingly call for less robust music, is a radical departure. Crew is situated in an alcove, or shell-like spot, which tends towards amplifying the output, and when mike pickup is added it reaches thunderous proportions. Good idea would be to cut off all amplifiers entirely, except for arrangements calling for an instrument to stand out, while the outfit is in the groove.

Webb's jive is smartly handled, however. During the dinner hours the jamming is curbed to smooth, listenable rhythm, which allows for almost ordinary conversation over the a la carte. After dinner, though, it's 'palm whacking in the palm room'. Outfit sends in jump style, and solid, with Webb situated out front at his skins. He beats 'em fast and furious, and the work of the 13 men behind him is aces. Instrumental setup of 12 pieces is split into four saxes, six brass and four rhythm and as a whole rates up there with the best in swing.

Ella Fitzgerald, who gets equal billing with the outfit, is tops. Her handling of any tune in any tempo seems so effortless, yet so much better than most of her contemporaries, that comparisons are impossible. This goes especially in her handling of the sequel to 'A-Tisket,' labeled 'I Found My Yellow Basket'. Delivered by Miss Fitzgerald, it's a sock tune. Same applies to the inevitable 'A-Tisket'. It's dated, but her interpretation, which was a best-seller record, gives it new life. 'Heart and Soul', 'FDR Jones,', 'What Do You Know About Love?' and 'St. Louis Blues' also click handsomely.

Four Inkspots, Derby Wilson, and a quintet from the band complete the short floor offering. Inkspots have been around and do an okay job here. Two of the four plunk a guitar and bass viol and add harmony while the other two handle main portion of the tunes. Mix 'em for variety and when caught clicked with exceptional arrangements of 'Timber', 'Who Stole My Heart Away?', 'Beautiful Baby,' and 'Thanks for Everything'. First and last are done solo by one. Impromptu terps and other spontaneous - appearing touches help.

Taps of Derby Wilson, augmented with announced attempts at Bill Robinson style, also clicks. Hoofer's work is acceptable, clear, and nicely varied in rhythm and pace. Robinson takeoff, though, could be slowed for better effect.

Bardou Ali waves the baton and m.c.'s. Does the latter smoothly and with dispatch and impresses favorably in front of the band. Fine cuisine, Webb's crew, and the natural appeal of a tastefully decorated room should combine to make this booking a profitable one all around.

Thursday 2 March 1939
Ella Fitzgerald records with the Chick Webb Orchestra for Decca in New York City.
ELLA FITZGERALD (vocal), DICK VANCE, TAFT JORDAN, BOBBY STARK (trumpets), SANDY WILLIAMS, NAT STORY, GEORGE MATTHEWS (trombones), HILTON JEFFERSON (alto sax), GARVIN BUSHELL (clarinet/alto sax), TED MCRAE (tenor sax), WAYMAN CARVER (tenor sax/flute), TOMMY FULFORD (piano), JOHN TRUEHEART (guitar), BEVERLY PEER (bass), CHICK WEBB (drums)
Sugar Pie (vEF) / *It's Slumbertime Along The Swanee* (vEF) / *I'm Up A Tree* (vEF) / *Chew-Chew-Chew (Your Bubble Gum)* (vEF)
Ella also records with her Savoy Eight.
ELLA FITZGERALD (vocal), TAFT JORDAN (trumpet), SANDY WILLIAMS (trombone), HILTON JEFFERSON (alto sax), TEDDY MCRAE (tenor sax/baritone sax), TOMMY FULFORD (piano), JOHN TRUEHEART (guitar), BEVERLY PEER (bass), CHICK WEBB (drums)
Once Is Enough For Me / *I Had To Live And Learn*

Ella Won't Wed

New York—Ella Fitzgerald isn't going to be married—at least anytime in the near future.

The diamond ring she is sporting of late is a Christmas gift of Moe Gale, her personal manager, and not symbolic of a betrothal promise, she says. All along the route, before she and Chick Webb's band moved into the Park Central here, Ella denied she was to be married but at the same time, would not comment on the diamond she sported. Now the truth is out and Ella herself swears the marriage angle is a false tip.

Saturday 4 March 1939
Ella Fitzgerald and the Chick Webb Orchestra are at the Amusement Area of New York World's Fair in Flushing, New York for the ground-breaking ceremony for what will become the fair's Savoy ballroom site.

Chick Webb and Erskine Hawkins' orchestras played before a crowd of five-hundred "jitterbugs" from Harlem for about an hour. Preceding this was Ella Fitzgerald's singing of the "Star Spangled Banner". New York's World Fair proper opens April 30, 1939.

Wednesday 8 March 1939
Ella Fitzgerald and the Chick Webb Orchestra open a two-week engagement at the Paramount Theatre in New York City. Also on the bill are The Southernaires, The Two Zephyrs and the Savoy Lindy Hoppers. The movie presentation is 'Never Say Die' starring Martha Raye and Bob Hope.

Tuesday 21 March 1939
Ella Fitzgerald and the Chick Webb Orchestra close at the Paramount Theatre in New York City.

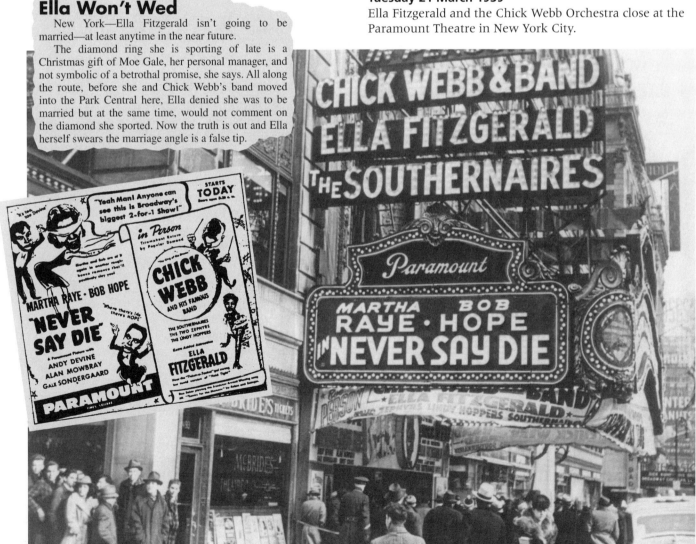

Thursday 23 March 1939
Ella Fitzgerald and the Chick Webb Orchestra play a one-nighter at the Paramount Theatre in Springfield, Massachusetts.

Friday 31 March 1939
Ella Fitzgerald and the Chick Webb Orchestra open a one-week engagement at the Howard Theatre in Washington, D.C. Also on the bill is Peg Leg Bates.
Before the opening Chick Webb enters the Johns Hopkins Hospital in Baltimore for an operation to drain the fluid in his back that has been causing him severe pain. Kaiser Marshall deputises on drums.

Thursday 6 April 1939
Ella Fitzgerald and the Chick Webb Orchestra close at the Howard Theatre in Washington, D.C.

Webb Feeling Better

Discharged from Johns Hopkins Hospital in Baltimore after a checkup which saw him leaving his band temporarily, Chick Webb returned and will be okay when the Webb men go back into the Park Central in N. Y. next month for a repeat date…

Friday 7 April 1939
Ella Fitzgerald and the Chick Webb Orchestra open a one-week engagement at the Royal Theatre in Baltimore, Maryland. Also on the bill is Peg Leg Bates. Chick Webb is reportedly back on drums for this engagement.

Thursday 13 April 1939
Ella Fitzgerald and the Chick Webb Orchestra close at the Royal Theatre in Baltimore, Maryland.

Friday 14 April 1939
Ella Fitzgerald and the Chick Webb Orchestra open a one-week engagement at the Fox Theatre in Philadelphia. Also on the bill is Peg Leg Bates and Chuck & Chuckles.

FOX, PHILLY

Philadelphia, April 14.
Chick Webb's orch, Ella Fitzgerald, Chuck & Chuckles, Pegleg Bates, Adolph Kornspan's house band; 'Society Lawyer' (M-G).

Fox this sesh goes sepia all the way and scores another click with a well-rounded and highly entertaining bill. Its weakness, if anything, is that it's not quite kept in hand enough by the m.c., front man for the Chick Webb crew. At final show (the fourth) on opening day, it was still running a little overboard on time and being slowed down by an overwillingness of the baton-waver to accede too easily to the demand for repeated encores.

Band is strong from the get-away right through to the finale and is given plenty to do. Swell Congo set provided by the house aids in the reception at the tee-off. Opener is 'Royal Garden Blues' and then Webb's own 'In the Groove at the Grove'. They serve nicely to introduce the various soloists and choirs, and also to bring out Webb's artistry on the traps. Neat harmony arrangement of 'Stompin' at the Savoy' follows, with the bass fiddle, drums, piano, clarinet and flute providing a quintet. Sweet flute work is highly unusual and outstanding in a band of this type.

Band itself, with its 14 pieces, seems to have toned down somewhat from previous appearances here. There is still plenty of the racy jive for which the outfit is noted, but there's also plenty of the sweeter side of swing and less pounding of raw brass. Webb, of course, as usual, holds his place behind the traps, while the stick-swishing and m.c.ing is handled by a personable sub.

Chuck and Chuckles, comedy pair, are in next. One lad's in a dudish suit and derby that's good for a snicker right off, while the other works on the lazybones order of Stepin Fetchit. Latter combines his molasses-like locomotion with rubber legs to good effect for laughs. Also gets in some terping with his partner after the boys warble 'We Were Born to Swing'. Pair encore with one working on a xylophone while the other dances. A fairly good turn now, it could be improved by holding it down in length and providing something stronger for the bows. Following Webb's rendition of

'Ragging the Scale, Pegleg Bates puts in his appearance. One-legged terper opens with a pattered bit of introduction before going into his dance. Combines straight tapping with a bit of acro stuff and a lesson in terping, all strong for audience appeal. Works well, too, with the m.c. and gets in a nice stunt of balancing on the artificial pin. Bates weakens his turn, however, with a continual and rather loose line of chatter. It's not very bright and sometimes gets too lengthy and annoying.

Ella Fitzgerald is more vivacious than ever, if that's possible, and is coutouriered better than usual. Takes off with 'Hold Tight,' then 'Heart Belongs to Daddy,' 'Ain't What You Do' and 'Undecided,' all naturals for her type of pipes. Her fluidity of style and bell-like pronunciation are swell.

Crew closes with a tremendous pot of jam medley that includes 'St. Louis Blues' and 'Tutti Fruiti,' Ella warbling. It provides a fine flash for the curtain.   *Herb.*

Thursday 20 April 1939

Ella Fitzgerald and the Chick Webb Orchestra close at the Fox Theatre in Philadelphia.

Friday 21 April 1939

Ella Fitzgerald records with the Chick Webb Orchestra for Decca in New York City.

ELLA FITZGERALD (vocal); DICK VANCE, TAFT JORDAN, BOBBY STARK (trumpets); SANDY WILLIAMS, NAT STORY, GEORGE MATTHEWS (trombones); HILTON JEFFERSON (alto sax); GARVIN BUSHELL (clarinet/alto sax); TED McRAE (tenor sax); WAYMAN CARVER (tenor sax/flute); TOMMY FULFORD (piano); JOHN TRUEHEART (guitar); BEVERLY PEER (bass); CHICK WEBB (drums)
Have Mercy (vEF) / *Little White Lies* (vEF) / *Coochi-Coochi-Coo* (vEF) / *That Was My Heart* (vEF)
Ella also records with her Savoy Eight.
ELLA FITZGERALD (vocal); TAFT JORDAN (trumpet); SANDY WILLIAMS (trombone); HILTON JEFFERSON (alto sax); TEDDY McRAE (tenor/baritone sax); TOMMY FULFORD (piano); JOHN TRUEHEART (guitar); BEVERLY PEER (bass); CHICK WEBB (drums)
Don't Worry 'Bout Me / *If Anything Happened To You* / *If That's What You're Thinking* / *If You Ever Change Your Mind*

Monday 24 April 1939

Ella Fitzgerald and the Chick Webb Orchestra open a two-week engagement at the Southland Café in Boston. On opening night, Ella and Chick broadcast from the Southland (8:15 to 8:30pm) via WAAB over the NBC network.

Tuesday 25 April 1939

Ella celebrates her 21st birthday in a photo booth (*below*).

Thursday 27 April 1939

Ella Fitzgerald and the Chick Webb Orchestra broadcast from the Southland (8:00 to 8:30pm) via WAAB over the NBC network.

Monday 1 May 1939
Ella Fitzgerald and the Chick Webb Orchestra broadcast from the Southland (8:00 to 8:30pm) via WAAB over the NBC network.

Chick Webb played a new tune on Monday night during his Southland broadcast of May 1st. The title of the original was "A Study in Grey," but changed to the name "Southland Shuffle" for his last broadcast.

Thursday 4 May 1939
Ella Fitzgerald and the Chick Webb Orchestra broadcast from the Southland (12:30 to 1:00am) via WAAB over the NBC network.
ELLA FITZGERALD (vocal), DICK VANCE, TAFT JORDAN, BOBBY STARK (trumpets), SANDY WILLIAMS, NAT STORY, GEORGE MATTHEWS (trombones), HILTON JEFFERSON (alto sax), GARVIN BUSHELL (clarinet/alto sax), TED McRAE (tenor sax), WAYMAN CARVER (tenor sax/flute), TOMMY FULFORD (piano), JOHN TRUEHEART (guitar), BEVERLY PEER (bass), CHICK WEBB (drums)
Let's Get Together (theme) / *Poor Little Rich Girl* / *Break 'Em Down* / *If I Didn't Care* (vEF) / *The Stars And Stripes Forever* / *My Wild Irish Rose* / *Chew-Chew-Chew (Your Bubble Gum)* (vEF)

Chick Webb and Ella Fitzgerald's introduction of *Chew, Chew, Chew Your Bubble Gum* in Boston brought a first order of 750 copies and phono-platters from beantown. Exclusive Publications ground it out, attaching slices of bubble gum to each copy.

Friday 5 May 1939
Ella Fitzgerald and the Chick Webb Orchestra broadcast from the Southland (8:00 to 8:30pm) via WAAB over the NBC network.

Saturday 6 May 1939
Ella Fitzgerald joins Roy Eldridge, Albert Ammons, the Jack Hill Orchestra and radio star Hildegarde for the Annual Harvard Freshman Smoker at the Sander's Theatre, Harvard University in Cambridge, Mass. Ella sings *Hold Tight* and *T'ain't What You Do, It's The Way That You Do It* before rejoining Chick Webb at the Southland Café.

Monday 8 May 1939
Ella Fitzgerald and the Chick Webb Orchestra broadcast from the Southland (8:00 to 8:15pm) via WAAB over the NBC network.

Thursday 11 May 1939
Ella Fitzgerald and the Chick Webb Orchestra broadcast from the Southland (8:00 to 8:15pm) via WAAB over the NBC network.

Friday 12 May 1939
Ella Fitzgerald and the Chick Webb Orchestra broadcast from the Southland (8:00 to 8:15pm) via WAAB over the NBC network.

Saturday 13 May 1939
Ella Fitzgerald and the Chick Webb Orchestra broadcast from the Southland (9:30 to 9:45pm) via WNAC over the NBC network.

Monday 15 May 1939
Ella Fitzgerald and the Chick Webb Orchestra broadcast from the Southland (10:00 to 10:30pm) via WAAB over the NBC network.

Thursday 18 May 1939
Members of Chick Webb's Orchestra beat Ben Bernie's crew in a softball game on Boston Common. During the Southland engagement they play several games against other bands. Ella is a faithful rooter at all the games.

The locale of this column at present being Boston make a complaint quite opportune. How come NBC bands, coming from there on sustaining programs, are given such poor balances? Both Charlie Barnet and Chick Webb have received raw deals so far as transmission on their efforts go, especially the latter, whose band at times sounds pretty much like a bassist accompanied by a bunch of guys named Joe in the next room. Barnet's music, too, suffers from a similar misconception of just which instruments should predominate in a dance band. The music of both outfits is much too good to be ruined by such sloppy engineering!

Friday 19 May 1939
Ella Fitzgerald and the Chick Webb Orchestra broadcast from the Southland (8:00 to 8:15pm) via WAAB over the NBC network.

Saturday 20 May 1939
Ella Fitzgerald and the Chick Webb Orchestra close at the Southland Café in Boston, Massachusetts.

Sunday 21 May 1939
Ella Fitzgerald and the Chick Webb Orchestra open a 5-night engagement at the Savoy Ballroom in New York City closing on Thursday 25th. Benny Carter's Band play the matinee shift from 6 to 8.00pm and Chick takes over at 8.30pm.

Friday 26 May 1939
Ella Fitzgerald and the Chick Webb Orchestra open a one-week engagement at the Apollo Theatre in New York City. Also on the bill are Willie Jackson & Son, Evelyn Keyes and Jackie 'Moms' Mabley. A substitute drummer, probably Bill Beason, plays part of the show.

Monday 29 May 1939
Ella Fitzgerald and Chick Webb make guest appearances in the large Swing Concert at the Hippodrome in New York .

APOLLO, N. Y.

Chick Webb orch (16), Ella Fitzgerald, Bardui Ali; Millie & Billie, Tenner & Swift, Jackie Mabley, Evelyn Keyes, Willie Jackson, Sr., Willie Jackson, Jr., Vivian Harris, Don Pierson; 'Bulldog Drummond's Secret Police' (Par.).

Apollo has another b.o. layout this week in Ella Fitzgerald and Chick Webb's band. Supporting lineup for Webb-Fitzgerald is not so strong, except in the comedy of Jackie Mabley, but the former pair are the draw.

In a familiar setting of drops splashed with musical notes, Webb doesn't get going on his own until late, early part of the 90-minute show being played from behind a scrim, with a substitute for Webb on the skins. Band's tee-off is an attractive swing arrangement of 'Stars and Stripes,' supplemented by an inspired layout of the new hit, 'Sunrise Serenade.' Sock swing version of 'My Wild Irish Rose' spotlights Webb's drum ability.

The band is on for fully 15 minutes before Miss Fitzgerald appears. The customers at this catching then didn't want to let her go. Her getaway is a rhythmic original, 'Peek-a-Boo.' Mixes 'em up neatly, following with 'Angels Sing,' another original; 'I'm in the Groove,' 'Don't Worry About Me' and 'Chew, Chew Your Bubble Gum,' last a whacky novelty along the lines of 'Three Fishies.' Bardui Ali leads the band and announces well.

Millie and Billie are a colored dance team featuring back-to-back terps that don't mean much. Forepart of the turn finds the two in unison taps that are mostly drowned out by the band. Tenner and Swift are standard rope tossers with little out of the ordinary. Highlight is a 55-foot lariat whirl, with the spinner on his back. Rest is the usual stepping in and out of spinning ropes. Exit, however, is speedy.

Jackie Mabley's the comedy strength and clicks solidly, utilizing 'T'ain't What You Do,' a setup for inserting original double entendre lyrics. Fade is a clever impromptu terps shuffle, which brings her back by demand for more.

Various settings for the production numbers are on the whole okay. Entire company works in an opening piece that's rather lengthy, followed by a blue piece between Miss Mabley and Willie Jackson, Jr., built around golf. Jackson Jr. and Sr. do a bit later that draws favorable response. Sing 'Small Fry' and follow with unison and challenge terps that earn 'em applause.

Standout production is an Indian setting built around 'Indian Love Call,' first done straight, then in swing. Don Pierson's unimpressive pipes warble the number. Evelyn Keyes works in several of the skits, her best contribution coming prior to the Webb portion, wherein she imitates the taps of Will Mahoney, Bill Robinson. et al. Footwork smoothly executed. Vivian Harris is a house standard, working in a bit during the opening sketch.

Left: Variety *reviews the show at the Apollo Theatre.*

Thursday 1 June 1939
Ella Fitzgerald and the Chick Webb Orchestra close at the Apollo Theatre in New York City.

Friday 2 June 1939
Ella Fitzgerald and the Chick Webb Orchestra play a one-nighter at the Suburban Gardens in Washington, D.C. Chick is ill and only able to play part of the evening. Drummer Kaiser Marshall substitutes.

Saturday 3 June 1939
Ella Fitzgerald and the Chick Webb Orchestra play two cruises (8.45pm and 12.30am) on the S. S. Potomac in Washington, D.C. Chick is ill and only able to play part of the evening. Drummer Kaiser Marshall substitutes.

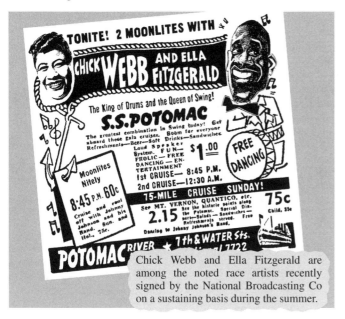

Chick Webb and Ella Fitzgerald are among the noted race artists recently signed by the National Broadcasting Co on a sustaining basis during the summer.

Sunday 4 June 1939
Members of the Chick Webb Orchestra join local talent for an evening jam session (6.00pm–9,00pm) at the Republic Café in Washington, D.C.

Friday 9 June 1939
Chick Webb enters the Johns Hopkins Hospital in Baltimore.

Sunday 11 June 1939
Ella Fitzgerald and the Chick Webb Orchestra play a one-nighter at Seaside Park in Norfolk, Virginia.

Monday 12 June 1939
Ella Fitzgerald and the Chick Webb Orchestra play a one-nighter at the Township Auditorium in Columbia, South Carolina.

Wednesday 14 June 1939
Ella Fitzgerald and the Chick Webb Orchestra play a concert and dance (8.30pm until 1.00am) at the City Auditorium in Atlanta, Georgia.

BRONZEMEN
—Presents—
The King of the Drums
CHICK WEBB and his Orchestra
Featuring
The first lady of swing
ELLA FITZGERALD
Township Auditorium, Mon. nite
June 12th

Advance 91c
Adm. at door $1.20
White spectators, Adv. 60c
Door 75c
Advance tickets on sale at Auditorium

J Neal Montgomery
Presents
The "King of the Drums"
CHICK WEBB
and His Famous Savoy Ballroom Band
Featuring the Nation's Most Popular Swing Singer
ELLA FITZGERALD
Composer of the Season's Most Outstanding Hit
"A TISKET - A - TASKET"
AT MACON AUDITORIUM
Thursday, June 15, 8:30 P. M.
Tickets go on sale at Fat Jack's Subway, 363 Broadway and Col. Dept. Macon Telegraph, Tuesday

Thursday 15 June 1939
Ella Fitzgerald and the Chick Webb Orchestra play a concert and dance (8.30pm until 1.00am) at the Macon Auditorium in Macon, Georgia.

Friday 16 June 1939
Chick Webb dies in Johns Hopkins Hospital in Baltimore.

Ella and the band are appearing at a dance at the Elk's Auditorium in Montgomery, Alabama. Having been travelling all day, the band know nothing of Chick's death until 60 minutes into the performance. Immediately they play *Taps*, followed by *My Buddy*. The rest of the southern tour is cancelled and Ella and the band make their way back (via New York) to Baltimore for the funeral.

Coming in Person!
The King of DRUMS
CHICK WEBB
America's Greatest
SWING BAND
With
ELLA FITZGERALD
SATURDAY NIGHT
9 P M Till 1 A M
City AUDITORIUM
TICKETS NOW AT
PARAMOUNT CIGAR STORE
ADVANCE   LAST DAY
Per Person, 85c   Per Person, $1.15
Colored Gallery, 40c
All Prices Include Tax

Chick Webb, Just Hitting Peak, Dies at 30 Following Operation

Chick Webb, 30, standout Negro drummer and orchestra leader, died June 16 in Johns Hopkins Hospital, Baltimore. Death followed an operation for kidney ailment from which he suffered for some time, and which forced him to desert his outfit on several occasions lately for short hospital sojourns. Invariably it was Johns Hopkins, where he spent a week recently while his band played a date at a Baltimore theatre. Burial was in Baltimore yesterday (Tuesday). Survived by widow, mother and two sisters. He was born there Feb. 10, 1909.

It's ironical that Webb died just a year or so after hitting the big time with his band. Fairly well known since first coming to New York in 1926, Webb didn't reach the peak of his popularity until then and a great deal of it hinged on his and Ella Fitzgerald's penning of 'A-Tisket A-Tasket' which started a cycle of nursery rhyme swing tunes. His first band was formed when he was about 17. Black Bottom Club was Webb's first New York date which was followed by the Paddock Club. Signed by Moe Gale, who was his manager still at death, Webb then went into Harlem's Savoy Ballroom. While playing there he heard Ella Fitzgerald singing in an amateur night at the Apollo theatre, in Harlem, and adopted her. She was an orphan.

Future of Band

While Moe Gale hasn't any plans for the future of Webb's band as yet, it's understood that it will remain together and may perpetuate the name of its leader by continuing as Chick Webb's orchestra. It's been said also that it may be listed—Ella Fitzgerald with Chick Webb's orchestra. It will be withdrawn from current commitments (18 dates) though it may fulfill a scheduled date at Loew's State, New York, the week of July 6.

At the time of his death it had been planned to have Webb withdraw from active participation in the band and devote himself to directing its operations from behind a desk, handling arrangements, rehearsing it and sitting in on recording dates. Band was the first outfit to sign with Decca when that org was formed in 1935, and his platters have consistently been among the best sellers. As a songwriter he turned out several hits, among them 'You Showed Me the Way,' 'In a Crying Mood,' 'Holiday in Harlem' and collaborated with Edgar Sampson or the now standard 'Stompin' at the Savoy.'

While at the Savoy, his drum work and the general advanced jive made the Harlem ballroom a Mecca for all musicians.

Tuesday 20 June 1939

Chick Webb's funeral takes place in Baltimore. Ella performs *My Buddy*, followed by Ms Lillian Matthews singing *I've Done My Work*. Next is Bertha Rosedom performing *Night Must Fall*, followed by Teddy McRae's sax solo *The End Of A Perfect Day*. The services are conducted by Rev. Dr. H.E.Walden, assisted by Rev. J.M.Boston and Rev. S.H.Giles. The pallbearers are Ralph Cooper, Claude Hopkins, Willie Bryant, Teddy Hill and members of the Chick Webb Orchestra.

Will Ella Take Over Webb Ork?

New York—Ella Fitzgerald will probably take over the Chick Webb band, according to Moe Gale, personal manager. Situation requires very little changes inasmuch as Bardu Ali has always fronted the band while Chick remained in the background surrounded by his tubs.

Thousands, many of them musicians, attended Chick's final rights last week.

What Next For Ella Fitzgerald?

Now that the throbbin,' vibrant, electric drum beating of Chick Webb is stilled forever, naturally, the question arises as to where will Ella Fitzgerald cast her lot?

Will there be a rush of outstanding white name bands to sign the "First Lady of Swing?" Will she reconsider the offer made her some time ago by Benny Goodman? Will some colored name Band grasp the opportunity, or will she endeavor to carry on the work of her discoverer?

Critics the world over, versed in the art of modern music, have acclaimed her "First Lady of Swing" with a voice superbly fine enough to enhance the efforts of the finest

Ponders Future

ELLA FITZGERALD

swing band in the land. She and Chick formed the greatest combination in that field today.

Both came up on the harder side of this thing called life, and both made good.

SERVICE SOUGHT

Even wh'c Chick was alive, musicians the country over, both white and colored, were in the market for her services, but the "Peacock of Rhythm" showed her gratitude to her discoverer and teacher by passing up a salary of an amazingly high figure.

Ella felt she owed her present reputation entirely to the guidance, and unceasing activities of her guardian. and nothing could

persuade her to alter her association.

It is said that Benny Goodman, from whom Webb, in a spectacular battle of music, captured the title, King of Swing, went so far as to offer her $5000 to join his aggregation, but with Chick, Ella had realized her fondest dream—she was the voice sensation with the greatest swing band in the country.

Today in popularity, the girl that Webb brought up from scratch, is second to none. She has popularized such songs as "My Last Affair," "Good Night My Love," "You Showed Me The Way," "A Tisket, A Tasket," "Deep Purple," and countless others.

It was merely accidental that Chick found the queen to do right by his kingly syncopation.

Visiting the Apollo Theatre during the Amateur Hour one of his off afternoons, Webb heard her tearing her heart out while singing a song. The fatal gong sounded and Ella was yanked off the stage.

Turning to his personal manager, Webb said, "They don't think she's good but, she has every quality I am seeking. She has youth, abundant vitality, and above all else—freshness. Now I hope she is willing to be taught a few things."

EAGER STUDENT

When he talked with her, he found her not only willing, but eager to learn the musical ways of this strange little man who had waited many years for such a voice personality as hers.

From then on the life story of Ella Fitzgerald took on a different slant. She wasn't the little struggling amateur any more, but a first class pro, with the stamp of approval of the greatest swing master of the ages.

She starred for six months as top voice feature on the Lucidin radio half-hour and gained wide acclaim through her appearance on the Camel program with Goodman. She is also outstanding Decca artist.

Just wherever she cast her lot, it will be small wonder when she lifts her voice and sings the tune "You Showed Me The Way" she will be looking high up to the drummer — who showed her the way—Chick Webb.

Chick Webb's Will Probed; Beason Hired

New York— Chick Webb left an estate of approximately $15,000 according to letters of administration issued in Manhattan surrogate court last month. About $10,000 will go to his widow, Mrs. Sally Webb. The remainder will go to his mother, who lives in Baltimore.

With Bill Beason pounding the drums, Chick's band has continued where it left off when the mighty little leader died in June. Ella Fitzgerald is in charge of the crew and it's being billed as "Ella Fitzgerald's Chick Webb Band."

The band work for about a week at the Savoy to rest the band and break in the new drummer, Bill Beason.

Thursday 29 June 1939

Ella Fitzgerald and her Famous Orchestra record for Decca in New York City.

ELLA FITZGERALD (vocal), DICK VANCE, BOBBY STARK, TAFT JORDAN (trumpets), GEORGE MATTHEWS, NAT STORY, SANDY WILLIAMS (trombones), GARVIN BUSHELL (clarinet/soprano sax), HILTON JEFFERSON (alto sax), WAYMAN CARVER (alto sax/tenor sax/flute), TEDDY MCRAE (tenor sax/baritone sax), TOMMY FULFORD (piano), JOHN TRUEHEART (guitar), BEVERLY PEER (bass), BILL BEASON (drums)

Betcha Nickel / Stairway To The Stars / I Want The Waiter / That's All, Brother / Out Of Nowhere

Thursday 6 July 1939

Ella Fitzgerald and her Orchestra open a one-week engagement at Loew's State Theatre in New York City. Peg Leg Bates and Chuck & Chuckles are also on the bill. The movie presentation is 'Wuthering Heights' starring Merle Oberon, Laurence Olivier and David Niven.

Wednesday 12 July 1939

Ella Fitzgerald and her Orchestra close at Loew's State Theatre in New York City.

Sunday 16 July 1939

Ella Fitzgerald and her Orchestra open a 6-week engagement at the Savoy Ballroom in New York City.

Monday 31 July 1939

Coleman Hawkins returns from Europe. On his first night back he and Benny Carter visit the Savoy Ballroom to hear Ella Fitzgerald and her Orchestra and Lee Norman's 9-piece jump outfit. Afterwards, Ella joins the party, now including Billie Holiday, Jimmy Lunceford, Charlie Shavers, Russell Procope and Buster Bailey, which drives down to 52nd Street to hear Basie at the Famous Door. At 4.30am they all drive up to Harlem's 'Jimmie's Chicken Shack.'

Friday 18 August 1939

Ella Fitzgerald and her Famous Orchestra record for Decca in New York City.

ELLA FITZGERALD (vocal), DICK VANCE, BOBBY STARK, TAFT JORDAN (trumpets), GEORGE MATTHEWS, NAT STORY, SANDY WILLIAMS (trombones), GARVIN BUSHELL (clarinet/soprano sax), HILTON JEFFERSON (alto sax), WAYMAN CARVER (alto sax/tenor sax/flute), TEDDY MCRAE (tenor sax/baritone sax), TOMMY FULFORD (piano), JOHN TRUEHEART (guitar), BEVERLY PEER (bass), BILL BEASON (drums)

My Last Goodbye / Billy / Please Tell Me The Truth / I'm Not Complainin' / Betcha Nickel

Wednesday 23 August 1939

Ella Fitzgerald guests on NBC radio's Red Network show 'George Jessel's Celebrities' in New York City. Jack Dempsey is also on the show.

Saturday 26 August 1939
Ella Fitzgerald and her Orchestra close at the Savoy Ballroom in New York City.

Monday 28 August 1939
Ella Fitzgerald and her Orchestra play an afternoon concert at the Revere Plaza in Revere, Massachusetts. In the evening they play a dance (9.00pm until 3.00am) at the Colonial Casino in Onset, Massachusetts.

Tuesday 29 August 1939
Ella Fitzgerald and her Orchestra play a dance (9.00pm until 2.00am) for Dining Car Employees at the Roseland State Ballroom in Boston, Massachusetts.

Saturday 3 September 1939
Ella Fitzgerald and her Orchestra play a dance at the Broadway Auditorium in Buffalo, New York.

Ella Fitzgerald Draws in Upstate Dance Appearance

JAMESTOWN, N. Y.—A total of 1,386 packed in Celeron Park's pier ballroom to hear Ella Fitzgerald and her orchestra. The advance sale grossed $250, 250 couples at $1. Box office sales mounted to 448 couples and the gate gross was $664.50 with total receipts hitting $914.50.

On the other hand, Claude Hopkins, playing the same spot a week before, drew only 834 dancers at a dollar a pair. In Buffalo, Ella drew a gross take of $950 at a dance at the Broadway Auditorium. Advance tickets were six bits with a buck a head at the door.

Saturday 9 September 1939
Ella Fitzgerald and her Orchestra play a dance at the Memorial Hall in Dayton, Ohio.

Sunday 17 September 1939
Ella Fitzgerald and her Orchestra play a dance at the Savoy Ballroom in Chicago.

To Chicago... Ella Fitzgerald brings her band into Ed Fox' Grand Terrace nitery September 18, first location job for the band in the Windy City in two years. Chick Webb's name has been dropped and the crew now is known simply as "Ella Fitzgerald and her Orchestra." Bill Beason is the drummer who has been moved back from Webb's front seat to the rear row and Bardu Ali remains front man. Ella has a Local 802 card now and is a full-fledged baton-handler.

Thursday 21 September 1939
Ella Fitzgerald and her Orchestra, after some confusion over the opening date, open a long engagement at the Grand Terrace in Chicago.

Ella Not Married
Ella Fitzgerald is NOT married to Leonard Reed, producer of the Grand Terrace shows...

Saturday 30 September 1939
After work at the Grand Terrace, Ella Fitzgerald joins Earl Hines and Eddie 'Rochester' Anderson in a 'swing jam' breakfast at LaRue's Tavern in Chicago.

Monday 9 October 1939
Ella Fitzgerald and her Orchestra play the Mayor of Bronzeville Ball at the Grand Terrace in Chicago.

Thursday 12 October 1939
Ella Fitzgerald and her Famous Orchestra record for Decca in Chicago.
ELLA FITZGERALD (vocal); DICK VANCE, BOBBY STARK, TAFT JORDAN (trumpets); GEORGE MATTHEWS, NAT STORY, SANDY WILLIAMS (trombones); GARVIN BUSHELL (clarinet/soprano sax); HILTON JEFFERSON (alto sax); WAYMAN CARVER (alto sax/tenor sax/flute); TEDDY MCRAE (tenor sax/baritone sax); TOMMY FULFORD (piano); JOHN TRUEHEART (guitar); BEVERLY PEER (bass); BILL BEASON (drums)
You're Gonna Lose Your Gal / After I Say I'm Sorry / Baby, What Else Can I Do? / My Wubba Dolly / Lindy Hoppers' Delight (instrumental) / *Moon Ray*

Saturday 28 October 1939
Ella Fitzgerald and her Orchestra close at the Grand Terrace in Chicago.

Sampson-Ella Riff; 'Too Many People'

New York—Edgar Sampson, director of the Ella Fitzgerald band, returned to New York unexpectedly a couple of weeks back declaring that "too many people" were trying to lead Ella's band.

"The boys were more interested in listening to ball games than in coming to rehearsals," said Sampson. Differences may be patched up but he'll stay here writing for the band instead of joining Ella on the road and working in the sax section, as he had been doing.

Sunday 5 November 1939
Ella Fitzgerald and her Orchestra play a farewell dance at the Savoy Ballroom in Chicago.

Thursday 9 November 1939
Ella Fitzgerald and her Orchestra play a dance at the Dreamland Ballroom in Omaha, Nebraska.

Thursday 23 November 1939
Ella Fitzgerald and her Orchestra play a one-nighter at the Cotton Club in Dayton, Ohio.

Friday 24 November 1939
Ella Fitzgerald and her Orchestra play a one-nighter at the Trianon Theatre in Cleveland, Ohio.
After some one-nighters, Ella and the Orchestra return to New York and go straight into Harlem's Savoy Ballroom opposite Erskine Hawkins' orchestra.

December 1939
Ella Fitzgerald and her Famous Orchestra broadcast from the Savoy Ballroom in New York City.
ELLA FITZGERALD (vocal), DICK VANCE, BOBBY STARK, TAFT JORDAN (trumpets), GEORGE MATTHEWS, NAT STORY, SANDY WILLIAMS (trombones), GARVIN BUSHELL (clarinet/soprano sax), HILTON JEFFERSON (alto sax), WAYMAN CARVER (alto sax/tenor sax/flute), TEDDY MCRAE (tenor sax/baritone sax), TOMMY FULFORD (piano), JOHN TRUEHEART (guitar), BEVERLY PEER (bass), BILL BEASON (drums)
A-Tisket, A-Tasket (theme) / Diga Diga Doo / 'Tain't What You Do / Breakin' Down / Oh, Johnny / Traffic Jam / Limehouse Blues / I Want The Waiter With The Water / Blue Lou / Confessin' / Swing Out

Sunday 24 December 1939
Ella Fitzgerald and her Orchestra play a concert (11.30pm until midnight) followed by a dance (until 4.00am) at the Roseland State Ballroom in Boston, Massachusetts. Their replacements at the Savoy for one night only are the all-conquering Glenn Miller Orchestra.

Monday 25 December 1939
Ella Fitzgerald and her Orchestra play a 3.00pm matinee at the Savoy Ballroom in New York City. Also appearing are Erskine Hawkins' Orchestra and the Savoy Sultans.

1940

Monday 1 January 1940

Ella Fitzgerald wins the *Down Beat* award for best female singer.

Shakeup Hits Ella's Band; Bob Stark Out

New York—Substantial changes in the Ella Fitzgerald personnel are being made. Bobby Stark, trumpeter, has already left and Irving "Mouse" Randolph, from Benny Carter's band, is in his chair.

"No more big bands for me," says Stark. "I will probably work with Kaiser Marshall's gang at the Victoria in Harlem, just to get my kicks."

Pneumonia Hits Fulford

Pianist Tommy Fulford, stricken with pneumonia, was rushed home, his place taken by "Ram" (Roger Ramirez), top-notch swing pianist who had only returned a couple of days before after several years in Europe.

Wayman Carver, saxist-arranger with the Fitzgerald band, was set to leave as soon as a replacement could be found, and chances were that trombonists Sandy Williams and Nat Story would be out before long.

Edgar Sampson Back

It is also expected that Edgar Sampson will again come into the band on fifth sax when Ella moves from the Savoy to the Famous Door shortly.

Monday 22 January 1940

Ella Fitzgerald and her Famous Orchestra broadcast from the Savoy Ballroom in New York City.

ELLA FITZGERALD (vocal), DICK VANCE, BOBBY STARK, TAFT JORDAN (trumpets), GEORGE MATTHEWS, NAT STORY, SANDY WILLIAMS (trombones), GARVIN BUSHELL (clarinet/soprano sax), HILTON JEFFERSON (alto sax), WAYMAN CARVER (alto sax/tenor sax/flute), TEDDY MCRAE (tenor sax/baritone sax), TOMMY FULFORD (piano), JOHN TRUEHEART (guitar), BEVERLY PEER (bass), BILL BEASON (drums)

A-Tisket, A-Tasket (theme) / Traffic Jam / A Lover Is Blue / Dodging The Dean / 'Tain't What You Do / I'm Confessin' / Blue Lou / What's The Matter With Me? / I Want The Waiter With The Water / Swing Out

Thursday 25 January 1940

Ella Fitzgerald and her Famous Orchestra broadcast from the Savoy Ballroom in New York City.

ELLA FITZGERALD (vocal), DICK VANCE, BOBBY STARK, TAFT JORDAN (trumpets), GEORGE MATTHEWS, NAT STORY, SANDY WILLIAMS (trombones), GARVIN BUSHELL (clarinet/soprano sax), HILTON JEFFERSON (alto sax), WAYMAN CARVER (alto sax/tenor sax/flute), TEDDY MCRAE (tenor sax/baritone sax), TOMMY FULFORD (piano), JOHN TRUEHEART (guitar), BEVERLY PEER (bass), BILL BEASON (drums)

A-Tisket, A-Tasket (theme) / Limehouse Blues / This Changing World / Oh, Johnny / Diga Diga Doo / Thank Your Stars / Take It From The Top / Vagabond Dreams / Breakin' It Up / Swing Out

Friday 26 January 1940

Ella Fitzgerald and her Famous Orchestra record for Decca in New York City.

ELLA FITZGERALD (vocal), DICK VANCE, BOBBY STARK, TAFT JORDAN (trumpets), GEORGE MATTHEWS, NAT STORY, SANDY WILLIAMS (trombones), GARVIN BUSHELL (clarinet/soprano sax), HILTON JEFFERSON (alto sax), WAYMAN CARVER (alto sax/tenor sax/flute), TEDDY MCRAE (tenor sax/baritone sax), TOMMY FULFORD (piano), JOHN TRUEHEART (guitar), BEVERLY PEER (bass), BILL BEASON (drums)

Is There Somebody Else? / Sugar Blues / The Starlit Hour / What's The Matter With Me?

End of January 1940: Alto saxist Chauncey Haughton and trombonist Claude Jones join Ella's band from Cab Calloway.

Monday 12 February 1940

Ella Fitzgerald and her Orchestra play a Webb Memorial Benefit at the 5th Regiment Armory in Baltimore, Maryland. Louis Armstrong is also on the bill.

Thursday 15 February 1940

Ella Fitzgerald and her Famous Orchestra record for Decca in New York City.

ELLA FITZGERALD (vocal), DICK VANCE, IRVING RANDOLPH, TAFT JORDAN (trumpets), GEORGE MATTHEWS, JOHN HAUGHTON, SANDY WILLIAMS (trombones), EDDIE BAREFIELD (clarinet/alto sax), CHAUNCEY HAUGHTON (clarinet/alto sax), SAM SIMMONS (tenor sax), TEDDY MCRAE (tenor sax/baritone sax), ROGER RAMIREZ (piano), JOHN TRUEHEART (guitar), BEVERLY PEER (bass), BILL BEASON (drums)

Busy As A Bee / Baby, Won't You Please Come Home? / If It Weren't For You / Sing Song Swing / Imagination

Tuesday 20 February 1940

Ella Fitzgerald and her Orchestra and Erskine Hawkins' Orchestra play an All Star Benefit Dance in aid of the Harlem Big Brother Association at the Renaissance Casino in New York City. Coleman Hawkins, Harlan Leonard, Claude Hopkins and many others are also there.

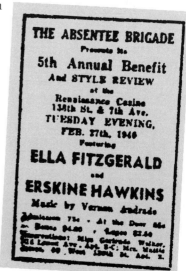

THE ABSENTEE BRIGADE
Presents the
5th Annual Benefit
And STYLE REVIEW
at the
Renaissance Casino
138th St. & 7th Ave.
TUESDAY EVENING,
FEB. 27th, 1940
Featuring
ELLA FITZGERALD
and
ERSKINE HAWKINS
Music by Vernon Andrade

Ella Fitzgerald and her Orchestra close at the Savoy and go into the Roseland Ballroom on Broadway.

Monday 26 February 1940

Ella Fitzgerald and her Famous Orchestra broadcast from the Roseland Ballroom in New York City.

ELLA FITZGERALD (vocal), DICK VANCE, IRVING RANDOLPH, TAFT JORDAN (trumpets), GEORGE MATTHEWS, JOHN HAUGHTON, SANDY WILLIAMS (trombones), EDDIE BAREFIELD (clarinet/alto sax), CHAUNCEY HAUGHTON (clarinet/alto sax), SAM SIMMONS (tenor sax), TEDDY MCRAE (tenor sax/baritone sax), ROGER RAMIREZ (piano), JOHN TRUEHEART (guitar), BEVERLY PEER (bass), BILL BEASON (drums)

Royal Garden Blues / Sing Song Swing / Sugar Blues (vEF) / *Sweet Sue / It's A Blue World* (vEF) / *Is There Somebody Else?* (vEF) / *One Moment Please* (vEF) / *I Wanna Be A Rug Cutter*

Tuesday 27 February 1940

Ella Fitzgerald and her Orchestra and Erskine Hawkins' Orchestra play a Benefit Dance in aid of the Absentee brigade at the Renaissance Casino in New York City.

Monday 4 March 1940

Ella Fitzgerald and her Famous Orchestra broadcast from the Roseland Ballroom in New York City.

ELLA FITZGERALD (vocal), DICK VANCE, IRVING RANDOLPH, TAFT JORDAN (trumpets), GEORGE MATTHEWS, JOHN HAUGHTON, SANDY WILLIAMS (trombones), EDDIE BAREFIELD (clarinet/alto sax), CHAUNCEY HAUGHTON (clarinet/alto sax), SAM SIMMONS (tenor sax), TEDDY MCRAE (tenor sax/baritone sax), ROGER RAMIREZ (piano), JOHN TRUEHEART (guitar), BEVERLY PEER (bass), BILL BEASON (drums)

A-Tisket, A-Tasket (theme) / *I Got Rhythm / One Cigarette For Two / Chewin' Gum* (vEF) / *Lover Come Back To Me / Who Ya Hunchin' / Sing Song Swing* (vEF) / *Goin' And Gettin' It / Make Believe / Starlit Hour* (vEF) / *Sign Off*

Below: Bandleader Russ Morgan visits Ella on the stand at the Roseland Ballroom in New York City. Ella looks very coy as trumpeter Taft Jordan waits to give the downbeat.

Wednesday 20 March 1940

Ella Fitzgerald and her Famous Orchestra record for Decca in New York City.

ELLA FITZGERALD (vocal), DICK VANCE, IRVING RANDOLPH, TAFT JORDAN (trumpets), GEORGE MATTHEWS, JOHN HAUGHTON, SANDY WILLIAMS (trombones), EDDIE BAREFIELD (clarinet/alto sax), CHAUNCEY HAUGHTON (clarinet/alto sax), SAM SIMMONS (tenor sax), TEDDY MCRAE (tenor sax/baritone sax), TOMMY FULFORD (piano), JOHN TRUEHEART (guitar), BEVERLY PEER (bass), BILL BEASON (drums)

Take It From The Top (instrumental) / *Tea Dance* / *Jubilee Swing* (instrumental)

late March 1940

Ella Fitzgerald and her Famous Orchestra broadcast from Roseland in New York City.

ELLA FITZGERALD (vocal), DICK VANCE, IRVING RANDOLPH, TAFT JORDAN (trumpets), GEORGE MATTHEWS, JOHN HAUGHTON, SANDY WILLIAMS (trombones), EDDIE BAREFIELD (clarinet/alto sax), CHAUNCEY HAUGHTON (clarinet/alto sax), SAM SIMMONS (tenor sax), TEDDY MCRAE (tenor sax/baritone sax), TOMMY FULFORD (piano), JOHN TRUEHEART (guitar), BEVERLY PEER (bass), BILL BEASON (drums)

A-Tisket, A-Tasket / *Diga Diga Doo* / *'Tain't Watcha Do* / *Breakin' Down* (instrumental) / *Oh Johnny, Oh! (VEF, TJ)* / *Traffic Jam* (instrumental) / *Limehouse Blues* (instrumental) / *I Want The Waiter* / *Blue Lou* (instrumental) / *I'm Confessin'* / *Swing Out* (instrumental)

Friday 22 March 1940

Ella Fitzgerald and her Orchestra open a one-week engagement at the Apollo Theatre in New York City. Also on the bill are Peg Leg Bates, Emil & Evelyn, The Two Zephyrs, Jackie 'Moms' Mabley and 16 Dancing Beauties.

Thursday 28 March 1940

Ella Fitzgerald and her Orchestra close at the Apollo Theatre in New York City.

Sunday 31 March 1940

Ella Fitzgerald and her Orchestra open another engagement at the Savoy Ballroom in New York City. Erskine Hawkins and his Band share the bill.

Saturday 13 April 1940

Ella Fitzgerald and her Orchestra close at the Savoy Ballroom in New York City.

Tuesday 16 April 1940

Ella Fitzgerald and her Orchestra open at the Famous Door in New York City.

Tuesday 23 April 1940

Ella Fitzgerald throws a gala party and is presented with her *Down Beat* trophy for best singer at the Famous Door in New York City.

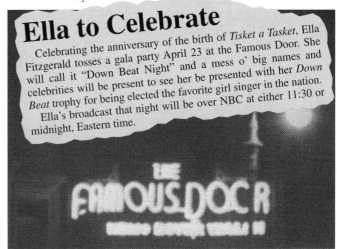

Ella to Celebrate

Celebrating the anniversary of the birth of *Tisket a Tasket*, Ella Fitzgerald tosses a gala party April 23 at the Famous Door. She will call it "Down Beat Night" and a mess o' big names and celebrities will be present to see her be presented with her *Down Beat* trophy for being elected the favorite girl singer in the nation. Ella's broadcast that night will be over NBC at either 11:30 or midnight, Eastern time.

Thursday 25 April 1940

Ella Fitzgerald's 22nd birthday.

Thursday 9 May 1940

Ella Fitzgerald and her Famous Orchestra record for Decca in New York City.

ELLA FITZGERALD (vocal), DICK VANCE, IRVING RANDOLPH, TAFT JORDAN (trumpets), JIMMY ARCHEY, FLOYD BRADY, JOHN MCCONNELL (trombones), PETE CLARK (clarinet/alto sax), CHAUNCEY HAUGHTON (clarinet/alto sax), SAM SIMMONS (tenor sax), TEDDY MCRAE (tenor sax/baritone sax), TOMMY FULFORD (piano), JOHN TRUEHEART (guitar), BEVERLY PEER (bass), BILL BEASON (drums)

Deedle-De-Dum / *Shake Down The Stars* / *Gulf Coast Blues* / *I Fell In Love With A Dream*

In the evening, Ella is a guest on John Kirby's radio show *Flow Gently, Sweet Rhythm*. Billie Holiday is also supposed to appear, but cancels when she realises Ella is a guest.

Tuesday 14 May 1940

Ella Fitzgerald and her Orchestra play a dance at the Roseland State Ballroom in Boston.

ESQUIRE CLUB
PRESENTS
ELLA
Fitzgerald
And Her
Orchestra
at the
Roseland State
Ballroom
TUESDAY,
MAY 14, 1940
Admission ---- $1.02
Tax Included

Wednesday 15 May 1940

Ella Fitzgerald and her Orchestra play a dance at Capitol Park in Hartford, Connecticut.

Ella-Benny Carter Combo Falls Through

New York—Despite several attempts to reorganize the Ella Fitzgerald setup, the band remained unchanged last week as Ella prepared for a long tour.

Several propositions were made to well-known arrangers to take charge of the band. Sy Oliver turned the offer down; Benny Carter was considering a deal which would have resulted in the disbanding of Ella's men, Ella joining forces with the Carter orchestra. Negotiations fell through and the Gale office will continue to run Carter and Fitzgerald as separate attractions, at least for the time being.

Ella Fitzgerald's band is going through a major underhauling. Pete Claud came in on 3rd alto replacing Eddie Barefield; Floyd Brady succeeded Sandy Williams on trombone and John McConnell also is a new sliphorn. Teddy McRae, Ella's tenor man, soon will take over the band as front man and director and Ella sticking only as vocalist. Meanwhile, Ella and Williams are still holding hands.

Alexander Baskerville
PRESENTS
ELLA
Fitzgerald
And Her
Orchestra
AT
CAPITOL PARK
Hartford, Conn.
WEDNESDAY,
MAY 15th, 1940
Dancing From 9:00 P.M.
Until 2 A.M.
Admission ---- $1.00

Throughout June, July and August Ella Fitzgerald and her Orchestra undertake a gruelling tour of one-nighters through the south and midwest.

Monday 1 July 1940

Down Beat reviews Ella's latest Decca release:

Ella Fitzgerald

"Lindy Hopper's Delight" & "Baby Won't You Please Come Home," Decca 3186

First side really jumps. Teddy McRae's tenor, a wonderful trombone (Sandy Williams?) and full-hard-biting brass blasts round out a well-turned performance. Ella sings only the "B" side. If nothing else, the tune is farmore listenable than most of the ones she's been recording of late. And she still knows how to sing. Not one in 100 other fem chanters approach Fitzgerald even when she's off form.

Washington DC Ella Fitzgerald's revamped outfit very impressive here.

Ella Fitzgerald Mobbed By Crowd; Clothes Ripped off

New Orleans—More than 4,000 Negroes, hysterical and in a panic mood, tore the clothes off Ella Fitzgerald late last month when she left the stand and made her way to an exit in the New Rhythm Club here following a one-nighter.

Many were knocked down, several were trampled and wild confusion reigned as hundreds of colored dancers rushed the "first lady of swing" for autographs. Police were called and attempted to maintain order. It was one of the largest crowds ever Assembled in this city for a "race" dance.

Ella and her band—the old Chick Webb group with a few changes—are touring the south. Ella was uninjured in the rush, but her gown was ripped and she escaped before the crowd could trample her underfoot.

Wednesday 17 July 1940

Ella Fitzgerald presents a Chick Webb Memorial Dance, featuring Louis Armstrong and his Orchestra, at the Arcanum State Ballroom in Boston.

Sunday 18 August 1940

Ella Fitzgerald and her Orchestra play a dance at the Savoy Ballroom in Chicago.

ONE NITE ONLY – SUNDAY, AUG. 18
SEE — HEAR IN PERSON
GALA DANCE
THE FIRST LADY OF SWING
ELLA Fitzgerald
AND HER famous ORCH
—ALSO—
FINAL CONTEST! – BEVY OF BATHING BEAUTIES
See Ella Crown "Miss Bronze Chicago"
$100.00 CASH TO WINNER!
SAVOY BALLROOM
So. Parkway at 47th St.

Saturday 24 August 1940

Ella Fitzgerald and her Orchestra play a one-nighter at the Fairground Coliseum in Dayton, Ohio.

CHICK WEBB MEMORIAL
DANCE
Gala Pre-Picnic Attraction
WED., JULY 17
$ $ CASH PRIZES $ $
AFRO-AMERICAN ASSOCIATES INC.
Presents
LOUIS ARMSTRONG
and his ORCHESTRA
MEMORIAL DEDICATION FLORAL OF MUSIC
Presented by
ELLA FITZGERALD
That lovable personality and Inimitable Queen of Syncopation
Recorded by Western Sound System
DANCING 9 TO 3 A.M.
Admission ---- 50c
(tax included)
Arcanum State Ballroom
423 Broadway, Everett Square
All Nite Transportation Service

Ella Goes 18,000 Miles Touring 36 States!

Detroit—Eighteen thousand miles through 36 states ain't exactly an overnight hike. Ella Fitzgerald and her boys feel it's something like a record on a one-nighter tour. They were winding up the trip here recently and were to jump off to New York to wax 26 sides within a single week for Decca. Tunes were to include Ella's own *Just One of Those Nights* and *Serenade to a Sleeping Beauty*, also DickVance's *I Solemnly Swear*.

Friday 13 September 1940
Ella Fitzgerald and her Orchestra open a one-week engagement at the Apollo Theatre in New York City. Also on the bill are Red & Curley, Sinclair & Leroy, John Mason & Vigal and Mary Bruce's Dancing Girls.

Ella elected to ASCAP!

Thursday 19 September 1940
Ella Fitzgerald and her Orchestra close at the Apollo Theatre in New York City.

Wednesday 25 September 1940
Ella Fitzgerald and her Famous Orchestra record for Decca in New York City.
ELLA FITZGERALD (vocal), DICK VANCE, IRVING RANDOLPH, TAFT JORDAN (trumpets), GEORGE MATTHEWS, EARL HARDY, JOHN MCCONNELL (trombones), PETE CLARK (clarinet/alto sax), CHAUNCEY HAUGHTON (clarinet/alto sax), SAM SIMMONS (tenor sax), TEDDY MCRAE (tenor sax/baritone sax), TOMMY FULFORD (piano), ULYSSES LIVINGSTON (guitar), BEVERLY PEER (bass), BILL BEASON (drums)
Five O'Clock Whistle / So Long / Louisville, KY

Tuesday 1 October 1940
Down Beat reviews Ella's latest Decca release and names her personnel as:
Chauncey Haughton, Pete Clark, Lonnie Simmons, Ted McRae (saxes), Dick Vance, Irving Randolph, Taft Jordan (trumpets), Jake Wiley, John McConnell, Earl Hardy (trombones), Tommy Fulford (piano), Beverly Peer (bass), Ulysses Livingston (guitar), Bill Beason (drums)

Gulf Coast Blues / Deedle-De-Dum (Decca 3324)
Ella's best vocal in two years—although inferior to Mildred Bailey's Vocalion and, of course, Bessie Smith's old Columbia, is *Gulf Coast*, the haunting old Clarence Williams blues made famous by Bessie in the early 1920's. Reverse means nothing. Both are all Ella, with the band getting little chance to show off.

Monday 7 October 1940
Ella Fitzgerald and her Orchestra open at the Savoy Ballroom in New York City.

Wednesday 9 October 1940
Ella Fitzgerald and her Orchestra broadcast from the Savoy Ballroom in New York City.

Friday 11 October 1940
Ella Fitzgerald and her Orchestra play a Scholarship Benefit Dance at the Savoy Ballroom in New York City. Also featured are the bands of Chris Columbus and Mercer Ellington.

Sunday 13 October 1940
Ella Fitzgerald and her Orchestra close at the Savoy Ballroom in New York City.

Friday 18 October 1940
Ella Fitzgerald and her Orchestra open a three-week engagement at the Tropicana, 1678 Broadway (the site that would later house Birdland), in New York City. Also featured are Socarras & his Rumba Orchestra, Mae Johnson, Avon Long, Swan & Lane, Flash & Dash and emcee Babe Wallace.

Thursday 7 November 1940

Ella Fitzgerald and her Orchestra close at the Tropicana in New York City.

New York—Bardu Ali's band replaced Ella Fitzgerald's at the Tropicana on Broadway last week. Ali is the man who fronted Chick Webb's band while Chick was alive. It's a sepia jump crew.

Friday 8 November 1940

Ella Fitzgerald and her Famous Orchestra record for Decca in New York City.

ELLA FITZGERALD (vocal), DICK VANCE, IRVING RANDOLPH, TAFT JORDAN (trumpets), GEORGE MATTHEWS, EARL HARDY, JOHN MCCONNELL (trombones), PETE CLARK (clarinet/alto sax), GEORGE DORSEY (alto sax), SAM SIMMONS (tenor sax), TEDDY MCRAE (tenor sax/baritone sax), TOMMY FULFORD (piano), ULYSSES LIVINGSTON (guitar), BEVERLY PEER (bass), BILL BEASON (drums)

Taking A Chance On Love / Cabin In The Sky / I'm The Lonesomest Gal In Town

Friday 27 December 1940

Ella Fitzgerald and her Orchestra open a one-week engagement at the Apollo Theatre in New York City. Also on the bill are Whitey's Dancers and Son & Sonny.

1941

Thursday 2 January 1941

Ella Fitzgerald and her Orchestra close at the Apollo Theatre in New York City.

Wednesday 8 January 1941

Ella Fitzgerald and her Famous Orchestra record for Decca in New York City.

ELLA FITZGERALD (vocal), DICK VANCE, IRVING RANDOLPH, TAFT JORDAN (trumpets), GEORGE MATTHEWS, EARL HARDY, JOHN MCCONNELL (trombones), PETE CLARK (clarinet/alto sax), GEORGE DORSEY (alto sax), SAM SIMMONS (tenor sax), TEDDY MCRAE (tenor sax/baritone sax), TOMMY FULFORD (piano), ULYSSES LIVINGSTON (guitar), BEVERLY PEER (bass), BILL BEASON (drums)

Three Little Words / Hello Ma! I Done It Again / Wishful Thinking / The One I Love (Belongs To Somebody Else) / The Muffin Man

Wednesday 19 February 1941

Ella Fitzgerald and her Orchestra open a one-week engagement at the Paramount Theatre in New York City. Also on the bill are Peg Leg Bates, Chuck & Chuckles and Bob Howard. The movie presentation is 'You're The One' starring Bonnie Baker, Jerry Colonna and Orrin Tucker & his Orchestra.

Tuesday 25 February 1941

Ella Fitzgerald and her Orchestra close at the Paramount Theatre in New York City.

Sunday 2 March 1941

Ella Fitzgerald and her Orchestra play a 3.00pm matinee dance at the Savoy Ballroom in New York City. Lucky Millinder and his Orchestra are also on the bill.

Friday 7 March 1941

Ella Fitzgerald and her Orchestra open a one-week engagement at the Howard Theatre in Washington, D.C.

Thursday 13 March 1941

Ella Fitzgerald and her Orchestra close at the Howard Theatre in Washington, D.C.

Monday 31 March 1941

Ella Fitzgerald and her Famous Orchestra record for Decca in New York City.

ELLA FITZGERALD (vocal), DICK VANCE, IRVING RANDOLPH, TAFT JORDAN (trumpets), GEORGE MATTHEWS, EARL HARDY, JOHN MCCONNELL (trombones), PETE CLARK (clarinet/alto sax), CHAUNCEY HAUGHTON (clarinet/alto sax), SAM SIMMONS (tenor sax), TEDDY MCRAE (tenor sax/baritone sax), TOMMY FULFORD (piano), ULYSSES LIVINGSTON (guitar), BEVERLY PEER (bass), BILL BEASON (drums)

Keep Cool, Fool / No Nothing / My Man

Friday 11 April 1941

Ella Fitzgerald and her Orchestra open a one-week engagement at the Apollo Theatre in New York City. Also on the bill are The King Brothers, Slim Thomas, Simpson's Humanettes, Bing Williams and Sterling & Rubia.

Thursday 17 April 1941

Ella Fitzgerald and her Orchestra close at the Apollo Theatre in New York City.

Friday 25 April 1941

Ella Fitzgerald's 23rd birthday.

Thursday 1 May 1941

Ella Fitzgerald and her Orchestra play a one-nighter at the Central Warehouse in Kingston, North Carolina.

Friday 2 May 1941

Ella Fitzgerald and her Orchestra play a one-nighter at the Jax Auditorium in Fayetteville, North Carolina.

Saturday 3 May 1941

Ella Fitzgerald and her Orchestra play a one-nighter in Rocky Mount, North Carolina.

Sunday 4 May 1941

Ella Fitzgerald and her Orchestra play a one-nighter in Valdosta, Georgia.

Friday 23 May 1941

Ella Fitzgerald and her Orchestra open a one-week engagement at the Regal Theatre in Chicago.

Thursday 29 May 1941

Ella Fitzgerald and her Orchestra close at the Regal Theatre in Chicago.

Monday 2 June 1941

Ella Fitzgerald and her Orchestra play a one-nighter in Kansas City. Drummer Jesse Price replaces Bill Beason as Ella and the band continue the tour, taking in Tulsa, Oklahoma on the way to Texas and then the West Coast.

Name Ballroom for 'Down Beat'

Tulsa, Okla.—A recently opened sepia ballroom in Tulsa was launched under the aegis of *Down Beat*. In the pic above, the take-off on the *Beat's* front cover title is seen above the band stand, with Ella Fitzgerald taking a chorus at the mike. Her band played a recent one-nighter at the spot. Ella arrived in Hollywood yesterday (30) to begin work in the new Abbott and Costello movie, "Ride 'Em Cowboy," in which she has a part. *Down Beat* pic by Cal Buckalew.

Ella and Ork To Tour Coast

Los Angeles—Ella Fitzgerald and band have been set for a tour of the west coast by the Reg D. Marshall office. Ella opens at the Orpheum Theatre here for a week starting June 26 and will continue from here on one-nighters and theatre dates.

Thursday 19 June 1941

Ella Fitzgerald and her Orchestra play a one-nighter at the City Auditorium in Houston, Texas.

Thursday 26 June 1941

Ella Fitzgerald and her Orchestra open a one-week engagement at the Orpheum Theatre in Los Angeles.

NOW! 4 STAGE SHOWS EVERY DAY
Orpheum
BDWY. NR. 9th • MI. 6272

Monday 30 June 1941

Ella Fitzgerald begins work on the Abbott & Costello movie 'Ride 'Em Cowboy' at Universal Studios in Hollywood.

Wednesday 2 July 1941

Ella Fitzgerald and her Orchestra close at the Orpheum Theatre in Los Angeles.

Ella Turned out to have so much talent in front of the cameras that the bigwigs at Universal have fattened her role with plenty of good lines and footage. Originally she had a relatively mediocre part as a colored maid. Also in the picture, "Ride 'em, Cowboy," are the Merry Macs, shown above going through a little jive with Fitzgerald. Ella revives *A-tisket A-tasket* in the pic, and also sings *Rockin' and Reelin'* with the Macs.

Ella Fitzgerald in New Movie

New York—Ella Fitzgerald went before Universal Studios' cameras June 30 on the coast for a featured part in the Abbott and Costello pic "Ride 'Em Cowboy." Although her band won't be seen in the film, Ella will sing as well as act. It's her first break on the screen.

The Fitzgerald outfit, formerly Chick Webb's, will be booked into a nitery in L.A., Ella fronting the band nights after finishing her movie stint in the daytime. Moe Gale, Fitzgerald's manager, set the deal here two weeks ago.

Tuesday 15 July 1941

Ella Fitzgerald and her Orchestra open a one-week engagement at the Trianon (formerly Topsy's) in Southgate, Calif. Ella doubles between the Trianon and Universal Studios where she is working on the Abbott & Costello movie.

Monday 21 July 1941

Ella Fitzgerald and her Orchestra close at the Trianon in Southgate, California.

Thursday 31 July 1941

Ella Fitzgerald and her Famous Orchestra record for Decca in Los Angeles.
ELLA FITZGERALD (vocal), DICK VANCE, IRVING RANDOLPH, TAFT JORDAN (trumpets), GEORGE MATTHEWS, EARL HARDY, JOHN MCCONNELL (trombones), PETE CLARK (clarinet/alto sax), CHAUNCEY HAUGHTON (clarinet/alto sax), SAM SIMMONS (tenor sax), ELMER WILLIAMS (tenor sax), TEDDY MCRAE (tenor sax/baritone sax), TOMMY FULFORD (piano), ULYSSES LIVINGSTON (guitar), BEVERLY PEER (bass), JESSE PRICE (drums)
I Can't Believe That You're In Love With Me / I Must Have That Man / When My Sugar Walks Down The Street / I Got It Bad / Melinda The Mousie / Can't Help Lovin' Dat Man

Jesse Price Quits Fitzgerald's Ork

St. Louis—Jesse Price, drummer-band leader who disbanded his own Kansas City jump outfit to take a job as hide-beater with Ella Fitzgerald's orchestra, quit the band here recently after an altercation with Ted McRae, tenor saxist.

One of the best known drummers in the Middlewest, Price, a former Harlan Leonard star sideman, who joined Fitzgerald after Ella persuaded him to abandon his own outfit, left the ork under Ella's protest. McRae has been rehearsing the band under Miss Fitzgerald's orders.

Sunday 31 August 1941
Ella Fitzgerald and her Orchestra play a dance at the Savoy Ballroom in Chicago.

They Liked It at Count Basie's Cafe Society opening last month, and Mrs. Jimmy Mundy, Jimmy, and Ella Fitzgerald show it plainly. Mundy, one of the finest jazz arrangers in the game, is now scribblin' 'em for the Count and the boys. *Harold Stein pic.*

Ella and the band return to New York for a week at the Famous Door on 52nd Street.

Friday 12 September 1941
Ella Fitzgerald and her Orchestra open a one-week engagement at the Apollo Theatre in New York City. Also on the bill are The Miller Brothers & Lois, Pansy the Horse, Myrtle Williams, Spider and Ashes & Johnny.

Tuesday 16 September 1941
After the show at the Apollo Theatre Ella Fitzgerald attends the Count Basie opening at Café Society Uptown in New York City. Harry James, Benny Goodman and Tommy Dorsey are also there.

Thursday 18 September 1941
Ella Fitzgerald and her Orchestra close at the Apollo Theatre in New York City.

Friday 19 September 1941
Ella Fitzgerald and her Orchestra open a one-week engagement at the Howard Theatre in Washington, D.C. Drummer Kenny Clarke joins the band for a five-week tour, but his stay is to be brief.

Thursday 25 September 1941
Ella Fitzgerald and her Orchestra close at the Howard Theatre in Washington, D.C.

Friday 26 September 1941
Ella Fitzgerald and her Orchestra open a two-week engagement at the Bermuda Terrace of the Hotel Brunswick in Boston. Trumpeter Dizzy Gillespie, recently fired from Cab Calloway's Band over the famous spit-ball incident, joins the band.

Bermuda Terrace Attraction
Ella Fitzgerald, the dusky darling of the dance world, opens the Bermuda Terrace of the Hotel Brunswick next Friday with her famous swing orchestra. Ella, just back from Hollywood, where she had an important role in Abbott and Costello's new comedy, "Ride Em, Cowboy," will bring to Boston, for the first time in modern cafe history, a 20th century streamlined minstrel show.

Monday 6 October 1941
Ella Fitzgerald records for Decca in New York City.
ELLA FITZGERALD (vocal), TEDDY McRAE (tenor sax), TOMMY FULFORD (piano), ULYSSES LIVINGSTON (guitar), BEVERLY PEER (bass), KENNY CLARKE (drums)
Jim / This Love Of Mine

Friday 10 October 1941
Ella Fitzgerald and her Orchestra are held over for a third week at the Bermuda Terrace of the Hotel Brunswick in Boston.

With her famous band, Ella Fitzgerald, America's renowned song bird, is performing to packed houses at the Bermuda Terrace of the Hotel Brunswick nightly…

Saturday 18 October 1941
Ella Fitzgerald and her Orchestra close at the Bermuda Terrace of the Hotel Brunswick in Boston. Teddy McRae is fired and Eddie Barefield takes over the responsibility of musical director. Dizzy Gillespie and Kenny Clarke leave the band. Drummer Bill Beason returns.

Barefield New Pilot of Ella Fitzgerald Ork

New York—Eddie Barefield, the Des Moines clarinettist who made good in the big time, returned to Ella Fitzgerald's band last month as leader, replacing Ted McRae, tenor saxist.

Barefield worked with Ella several years ago when the late Chick Webb led the band from his battery. Later, Eddie worked with Benny Carter and others. For a time he even had his own band.

He'll have complete charge of the band's rehearsals, songs and everything pertaining to the music end, while Miss Fitzgerald continues to handle the vocal assignments. Moe Gale's office booking.

Friday 24 October 1941
Ella Fitzgerald and her Orchestra open a four-week engagement at the Savoy Ballroom in New York City.

Ella's Song Squares But She Doesn't

Harry L. Flannery, who took Bill Shirer's post in Berlin when the latter came home to write *Berlin Diary*, is shown here with Ella Fitzgerald whom he sought out for congratulations upon his own return to the States. Flannery reported that the current song hit of *Aryan* Germany is the swing version of *A-Tisket A-Tasket*, written by the sepia songstress. But the real laugh on Hitler is that Ella herself doesn't square with Nazi definitions of Aryanism.

Tuesday 28 October 1941
Ella Fitzgerald records for Decca in New York City.
ELLA FITZGERALD (vocal), EDDIE BAREFIELD (alto sax), TOMMY FULFORD (piano), ULYSSES LIVINGSTON (guitar), BEVERLY PEER (bass), BILL BEASON (drums)
Somebody Nobody Loves / You Don't Know What Love Is

Wednesday 5 November 1941
Ella Fitzgerald records for Decca in New York City.
ELLA FITZGERALD (vocal), EDDIE BAREFIELD (alto sax), TOMMY FULFORD (piano), ULYSSES LIVINGSTON (guitar), BEVERLY PEER (bass), BILL BEASON (drums)
Who Are You? / I'm Thrilled / Make Love To Me

Saturday 15 November 1941
Ella Fitzgerald and her Orchestra play a dance at the Brooklyn Palace in Brooklyn, New York.

Ella Fitzgerald and her Orchestra on the stand at the Savoy Ballroom. Tommy Fulford (piano, out of shot); Beverly Peer (bass); Ulysses Livingstone (guitar); Bill Beason (drums); Ella; Eddie Barefield (clarinet/MD); Taft Jordan, Irving 'Mouse' Randolph, Dick Vance, Francis Williams (trumpets); John McConnell, Earl Hardy, George Matthews (trombones); Elmer Williams, Chauncey Haughton, Willard Brown, Lonnie Simmons (saxes).

Thursday 20 November 1941

Ella Fitzgerald and her Orchestra close at the Savoy Ballroom in New York City.

Ella and the band then set out on a long tour. For a long time Ella has been seeing a hanger-on called Benny Kornegay and he joins her on tour, sharing her room. She seems blind to his obvious faults and when he proposes marriage she readily agrees.

Bassist Beverly Peer remembered:

THAT'S WHO SHE WENT OFF WITH IN BETWEEN SHOWS. EVERYONE CALLED HIM CIGARETTE. I DON'T KNOW WHY; HE WASN'T TALL AND THIN. HE WAS A QUIET PRIVATE GUY.

Sunday 7 December 1941

Japanese aircraft attack the U.S. Fleet at Pearl Harbour in Hawaii and the US declare war on Japan.

Friday 26 December 1941

Ella Fitzgerald marries Benny Kornegay in St. Louis, Missouri. The Moe Gale Agency are horrified and, when they hear of the 'monetary discrepancies' attributed to Kornegay, they decide to have him investigated. They discover that he has a criminal record and has been jailed for drug offences. Ella is persuaded to drop him and the Gale office seek an annulment through the New York State judiciary.

1942

Friday 13 February 1942

Ella Fitzgerald and her Orchestra open a one-week engagement at the Apollo Theatre in New York City. Also on the bill are Bobby Evans, The Two Zephyrs, The Three Riffs, The Six Faludys and Moore & Byrd.

Thursday 19 February 1942
Ella Fitzgerald and her Orchestra close at the Apollo Theatre in New York City.

Wednesday 25 February 1942
Ella Fitzgerald and her Orchestra play a USO Camp Show at Fort Jay on Governor's Island in New York.

USO Camp Shows Feature La Ella

A ferryboat full of jive unloaded at Governor's Island, Wednesday, when Ella Fitzgerald, the golden girl of the dance business, took her famous orchestra for a USO-Camp Show volunteer playdate at Fort Jay.

The Tisket-Tasket Gal and her solid sending band of Harlem rhythm men are another of the nation's top dance and radio bands contributing their services to USO-Camp Shows who book them into camps and naval stations all over the country, where they play early evening performances free for Uncle Sam's service men.

The men stationed at Fort Jay got a chance to hear the famous Fitzgerald version of current hit tunes and such of her favorites as "You Showed Me The Way," "Goodnight My Love" and "I'm The Loneliest Gal In Town."

Thursday 26 February 1942
Ella Fitzgerald and her Orchestra play a one-nighter at the University of Michigan in Ann Arbor, Michigan.

Sunday 1 March 1942
Ella Fitzgerald and her Orchestra open a one-week engagement at the Plymouth Theatre in Worcester, Massachusetts.

Saturday 7 March 1942
Ella Fitzgerald and her Orchestra close at the Plymouth Theatre in Worcester, Massachusetts.

Wednesday 11 March 1942
Ella Fitzgerald and The Four Keys record for Decca in New York City.
ELLA FITZGERALD (vocal) accompanied by The Four Keys : BILL FURNESS (piano), SLIM FURNESS (guitar), PECK FURNESS (bass), ERNIE HATFIELD (drums/vocal)
I'm Getting Mighty Lonesome / When I Come Back Crying

Friday 13 March 1942
Ella Fitzgerald and her Orchestra open a one-week engagement at the Savoy Ballroom in New York City.

Thursday 19 March 1942
Ella Fitzgerald and her Orchestra close at the Savoy Ballroom in New York City.

Wednesday 25 March 1942
Ella Fitzgerald and her Orchestra play a dance at the Ritz Plaza Ballroom in Boston, Massachusetts.

Friday 27 March 1942
Ella Fitzgerald and her Orchestra open a one-week engagement at the Royal Theatre in Baltimore, Maryland.

Thursday 2 April 1942
Ella Fitzgerald and her Orchestra close at the Royal Theatre in Baltimore, Maryland.

Friday 3 April 1942
Ella Fitzgerald and her Orchestra open a one-week engagement at the Howard Theatre in Washington, D.C.

Thursday 9 April 1942
Ella Fitzgerald and her Orchestra close at the Howard Theatre in Washington, D.C.

Friday 10 April 1942
Ella Fitzgerald and The Four Keys record for Decca in New York City.
ELLA FITZGERALD (vocal) accompanied by TOMMY FULFORD (piano) and The Four Keys
All I Need Is You / Mama Come Home

Thursday 16 April 1942
Ella Fitzgerald and her Orchestra play a one-nighter at the Cleveland Coliseum in Cleveland, Ohio.

Friday 17 April 1942
Ella Fitzgerald and her Orchestra open a one-week engagement at the Buffalo Theatre in Buffalo, New York.

Thursday 23 April 1942
Ella Fitzgerald and her Orchestra close at the Buffalo Theatre in Buffalo, New York.

Friday 24 April 1942
Ella Fitzgerald and her Orchestra open a one-week engagement at the Regal Theatre in Chicago. Also on the bill is Erskine Butterfield and the movie presentation is "Remember The Day" starring Claudette Colbert and John Payne.

Saturday 25 April 1942
Ella Fitzgerald's 24th birthday.

Tuesday 28 April 1942
Ella Fitzgerald and other leading orchestra leaders, including Coleman Hawkins, Cootie Williams and Tiny Bradshaw, are entertained by Ed White of Ed White's Emporium in Chicago.

Thursday 30 April 1942
Ella Fitzgerald and her Orchestra close at the Regal Theatre in Chicago.

Ella with Band Part of Time

New York—Ella Fitzgerald is not completely severing connections with her band. Moe Gale, who does her booking, felt that it would be more profitable for her in the long run to stick in the New York area, doing club dates, radio, and record work with an instrumental combo, The Three Keys backing.

At present, the financial burden of a big band forces Ella to stay on the road most of the time, mixing one-nighters and theaters. Under present plans, Gale hopes to have Ella join the band for part of each year for dances and theater work. In the interim, the band will be booked as a separate unit under Eddie Barefield, sax-clary man, who some years ago fronted a crack West Coast combo.

Wednesday 13 May 1942
Ella Fitzgerald and her Orchestra open a four-week engagement at the Trianon Ballroom in Los Angeles.

Friday 15 May 1942
Down Beat reviews Ella's latest release:

Ella Fitzgerald with the Four Keys
I'm Getting Mighty Lonesome and *When I Come Back Crying*
Best Ella's done in some time but what a difference in her style! As compared with her singing with the Webb band, she's softened down, dropped her jump phrasing, and become almost a ballad singer. Four Keys sing like the Delta Rhythm Boys that Mildred Bailey used for some Decca dates, and play acceptable accompaniment. These are certainly far better sales bets than anything Ella has made in a year.

Ella Fitzgerald to Get Blue Build-up

New York—Ella Fitzgerald is slated shortly for a build-up on the Blue Network, with backing by the Four Keys, the group she's been using for records. In the interim, she's been working with Dolores Barefield, daughter of lead-saxist Eddie, who will front the band. Seems likely former will take Ella's place on the vocals.

Monday 1 June 1942
Down Beat reviews Ella's latest release:

Ella Fitzgerald
All I Need Is You and *Mama Come Home*
A nice job, this new Mitch Parish song, and Ella sings it properly. But Fitz fans will never recognize it as the singing of Chick's vocalist. In the past few months, her whole style has changed from driving rhythm phrases to almost lush ballad style. Flip-over is a sequel to *Five O'Clock Whistle*.

Wednesday 10 June 1942
Ella Fitzgerald and her Orchestra close at the Trianon Ballroom in Los Angeles.

Sunday 21 June 1942
Ella Fitzgerald and her Orchestra play a dance at the Savoy Ballroom in Chicago.

Thursday 25 June 1942
Ella Fitzgerald is a special attraction at a U.S.O. Benefit Dance at the Golden Gate Ballroom in New York City. The event features eight big bands and a host of special attractions.

Thursday 2 July 1942
Ella Fitzgerald and her Orchestra play a one-nighter at the City Auditorium in Houston, Texas.

Friday 3 July 1942
Ella Fitzgerald and her Orchestra play a one-nighter at the City Auditorium in Galveston, Texas.

Saturday 4 July 1942
Ella Fitzgerald and her Orchestra play a one-nighter at the City Auditorium in Dallas, Texas.

Sunday 5 July 1942
Ella Fitzgerald and her Orchestra play a one-nighter at the City Auditorium in Fort Worth, Texas.

Monday 6 July 1942
Ella Fitzgerald and her Orchestra play a one-nighter at the Library Auditorium in San Antonio, Texas.

Friday 10 July 1942
Ella Fitzgerald and her Orchestra play a one-nighter at the Cotton Club in Port Arthur, Texas.

Sunday 19 July 1942
Ella Fitzgerald and her Orchestra play a dance at the Savoy Ballroom in Chicago.

Monday 20 July 1942
Ella Fitzgerald and her Orchestra play a one-nighter at the Graystone Ballroom in Detroit, Michigan.

Tuesday 21 July 1942
Ella Fitzgerald and her Orchestra play a one-nighter at the St. Moritz in Pittsburgh, Pennsylvania.

Wednesday 22 July 1942
Ella Fitzgerald and her Orchestra play a one-nighter at the Chestnut Theatre in Harrisburg, Pennsylvania.

Friday 24 July 1942
Ella Fitzgerald and her Orchestra open a one-week engagement with dancer Bill 'Bojangles' Robinson at the Earle Theatre in Philadelphia, Pennsylvania. This is the last engagement by the big band.

Thursday 30 July 1942
Ella Fitzgerald and her Orchestra close at the Earle Theatre in Philadelphia, Pennsylvania. The big band breaks up and Ella begins a solo career.

First Lady of Swing Does Swan Song

Theatre marquees will no longer bill, "Ella Fitzgerald and her orchestra," as the aggregation did its swan song appearance at the Earle Theatre here.

Miss Fitzgerald joins the Four Keys for recordings in New York, just getting in under the deadline on new waxings, and if the possibility of a commercial air show materializes, the new combo will play night club and personal appearances around New York until they can safely plan for the future.

Fans Applaud Favorites

The First Lady's cooing of "Knock Me A Kiss" knocked the customers right out, and "A Tisket etc." still occupies a nook deep in the heart of swing fans. There is only one version of "Baby All I Need Is You," and when Ella went to work with her creamy tone and tricky phrasings, that's all brother.

Even the hackneyed "Johnny Doughboy" sounded "aw reet" as dispensed by Mrs. Swing's favorite daughter.

Band to Continue

The band musically protested any idea that they will lapse into obscurity, but definitely, and had the audience stomping, clapping, and one little jitterbug in the second row jumped up every now and then and gave out with bumps in perfect timing.

Eddie Barefield, front and center, took a few solos on his clarinet that were plenty solid. Joe Jordan on trumpet took sweet and hot in his stride, and every time Sonny Simmons and his sax were featured howls of approval rang out leaving no doubt as to what instrument is riding high on the crest of popularity.

Bojangles Still Tops

The Douglas Brothers made with the taps combining classic technique, boogie-woogie, and a zany routine that garnered several curtain calls. It's now "Brother Bill," Robinson, formerly "Bojangles," who still holds an audience in the palm of his hands, brushing off hecklers with the same ease with which he carries his sixty-four years.

His version of himself forty years from today brought the house down, and the only improvement we can suggest is the elimination of his "and the little colored boy said to the little white boy."

Friday 31 July 1942
Ella Fitzgerald and The Four Keys record for Decca in New York City.
ELLA FITZGERALD (vocal) accompanied by TOMMY FULFORD (piano) and The Four Keys
My Heart And I Decided / I Put A Four-Leaf Clover In Your Pocket / He's My Guy

Saturday 1 August 1942
Down Beat reviews Ella's latest release:

Ella Fitzgerald
I Can't Believe That You're In Love With Me and *Can't Help Lovin' That Man (Decca)*
Done with the big band, these are two more of Ella's new smooth-styled singing. It's good, better than a lot she's done lately; and the background on *Man* is as pretty as anything she's ever had. But the driving power that made Ella a great singer seems to have trickled away.

James Caesar Petrillo, of the American Federation of Musicians calls for a recording ban by his members.

September 1942

Ella Fitzgerald begins her solo career with the Four Keys with a short residency at the Aquarium Restaurant in Times Square, New York City.

Ella Takes Air

New York—Ella Fitzgerald's new Blue Network sustainer started last week, with two shows on Monday and Wednesday at 11:15 pm.

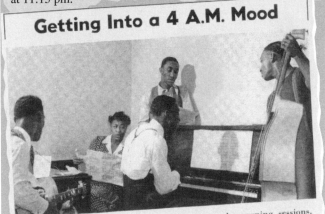

Getting Into a 4 A.M. Mood

New York—This looks like one of those early morning sessions, but it's broad daylight and Ella Fitzgerald and the Four Keys are knocking themselves out with a Blue Network rehearsal. Slim Furness is on guitar, brother Bill is at box, while also-brother Art plays bass. Ernie Hatfield just vocalizes.

Friday 18 September 1942
Ella Fitzgerald opens a two-week engagement at the RKO Theatre in Boston.

Thursday 1 October 1942
Ella Fitzgerald closes at the RKO Theatre in Boston.

Friday 16 October 1942
Ella Fitzgerald opens a one-week engagement at the Howard Theatre in Washington, D.C.

Thursday 22 October 1942
Ella Fitzgerald closes at the Howard Theatre in Washington, D.C.

Sunday 25 October 1942
Ella Fitzgerald and The Four Keys open a two-week engagement at the Tic Toc Club in Boston, Massachusetts.

Friday 6 November 1942
Ella Fitzgerald and The Four Keys close at the Tic Toc Club in Boston.

Saturday 14 November 1942
Ella Fitzgerald and The Four Keys play a one-night engagement at the Plaza Hotel in New York City.

Friday 20 November 1942
Ella Fitzgerald and The Four Keys open a one-week engagement at the Apollo Theatre in New York City. Also on the bill are The Savoy Sultans, Pee Wee the Midget, Atta Blake, Bobby & Foster Johnson and John Mason.

Thursday 26 November 1942
Ella Fitzgerald and The Four Keys close at the Apollo Theatre in New York City.

Friday 4 December 1942
Ella Fitzgerald and The Four Keys open a one-week engagement at the Royal Theatre in Baltimore, Maryland.

Thursday 10 December 1942
Ella Fitzgerald and The Four Keys close at the Royal Theatre in Baltimore, Maryland.

Friday 11 December 1942
Ella Fitzgerald and The Four Keys open a one-week engagement at the Paradise Theatre in Detroit.

Thursday 17 December 1942
Ella Fitzgerald and The Four Keys close at the Paradise Theatre in Detroit.

Friday 18 December 1942
Ella Fitzgerald and The Four Keys open a one-week engagement at the Oriental Theatre in Chicago. Also on the bill are Chuck Foster & his Orchestra. The movie presentation is "Secrets Of The Underground."

Thursday 24 December 1942
Ella Fitzgerald and The Four Keys close at the Oriental Theatre in Chicago.

Wednesday 30 December 1942
Ella Fitzgerald and Romo Vincent open a one-week engagement at Loew's State Theatre in New York City. The movie presentation is "A Night To Remember" starring Loretta Young and Brian Aherne.

1943

Tuesday 5 January 1943
Ella Fitzgerald closes at Loew's State Theatre in New York City.

Monday 15 February 1943
Down Beat reviews Ella's latest release:

> **Ella Fitzgerald**
> *I Must Have That Man / My Heart And I Decided*
> Another indication of how Ella has smoothed her style from her old Webb days. Maybe it's radio work, but she sings now in a complete ballad fashion, without any of the hard-bitten inflection that first made her famous. Not that this isn't good singing—it's just different. First side was made in Los Angeles, with the old band, while the second was done in NYC with the Keys.

Friday 26 February 1943
Ella Fitzgerald and The Four Keys open a one-week engagement at the Apollo Theatre in New York City. Also on the bill are Eddie Durham's All-Girl Band, The Wallace Brothers, The Great Bender, Allen Drew and Pigmeat Markham.

Thursday 4 March 1943
Ella Fitzgerald and The Four Keys close at the Apollo Theatre in New York City.

Ella and Four Keys move on to Philadelphia and, according to *Down Beat's* 15 March issue, are appearing at Club Bali and doubling at the Little Rathskeller.

Friday 26 March 1943
Ella Fitzgerald and The Four Keys open a one-week engagement at Fays Theatre in Philadelphia, Pennsylvania.

Thursday 1 April 1943
Ella Fitzgerald and The Four Keys close at Fays Theatre in Philadelphia, Pennsylvania.

Saturday 10 April 1943
Ella Fitzgerald and The Four Keys play a dance with Erskine Hawkins' Orchestra at the Royal Windsor in New York City.

Thursday 15 April 1943
Ella Fitzgerald and The Four Keys play a Star Spangled Concert at Symphony Hall in Boston. Also on the bill are the John Kirby Orchestra, The Boogie Woogie Pianists (Albert Ammons & Pete Johnson) and Una Mae Carlisle.

Sunday 25 April 1943
Ella Fitzgerald's 25th birthday.

Sunday 2 May 1943
Ella Fitzgerald and The Four Keys open a one-week engagement at the Howard Theatre in Washington, D.C.

Saturday 8 May 1943
Ella Fitzgerald and The Four Keys close at the Howard Theatre in Washington, D.C.

Friday 21 May 1943
Ella Fitzgerald and The Four Keys and the Sabby Lewis Band play a dance at the Roseland State Ballroom in Boston.

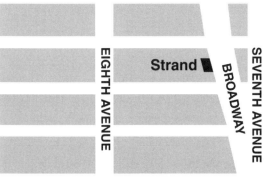

Sunday 30 May 1943
Ella Fitzgerald and The Four Keys and the Sabby Lewis Band play a dance at the Roseland Ballroom in Taunton, Massachusetts.

Monday 31 May 1943
Ella Fitzgerald and The Four Keys and the Sabby Lewis Band play a holiday dance at Egleston Square Gardens in Boston, Massachusetts.

Friday 18 June 1943
Ella Fitzgerald and The Four Keys open a one-week engagement at the Apollo Theatre in New York City. Also on the bill are Eddie Durham's All-Girl Band, Tim Moore and Peckin' Joe.

Thursday 24 June 1943
Ella Fitzgerald and The Four Keys close at the Apollo Theatre in New York City.

Thursday 8 July 1943
Ella Fitzgerald opens at the new night club, The Café Zanzibar, on Broadway between 50th and 51st Streets in New York City. Ella's new pianist and musical director is Bill Doggett. Also on the bill are the Berry Brothers, Moke & Poke, Avis Andrews, Maurice Rocco, Earle & Frances, Don Redman & his Orchestra and Canay and his Rumbas.

Ella Fitzgerald In Broadway Club

New York—Ella Fitzgerald opens at the new Zanzibar Club on Broadway tonight. The nitery, formerly the Frolics, has the reputation of being a jinxed spot, several promoters having flopped there. The Street is going to watch Ella's venture with superstitious interest.

Club Zanzibar Has Premiere

New York—Don Redman with a thirteen piece outfit, Ella Fitzgerald, and Maurice Rocco, boogie-woogie pianist, opened the new Club Zanzibar on Broadway one week ago.

Redman, well-known both as an arranger and bandleader, had to change his plans regarding certain side-men whom he planned to use in the band because of their lack of Local 802 cards. Instrumentation is four reeds, three trumpets, three trombones, and three rhythm and Mable Mayfair is the gal vocalist. Redman has written several new tunes which will be played for the first time at the Zanzibar, including one which has the intriguing title *You Don't Have to Go Home, But You've Got to Leave Here.*

Ella remains at the Café Zanzibar throughout July, August and September, and into October.

Wednesday 13 October 1943
Ella Fitzgerald closes at the Café Zanzibar in New York City.

Friday 15 October 1943
Ella Fitzgerald opens a one-week engagement at the Apollo Theatre in New York City. Also on the bill are Eddie Durham's All-Girl Band, Cowan's Cyclonic Musical Madcaps, The Bryants and Rubberlegs Williams.

Thursday 21 October 1943
Ella Fitzgerald closes at the Apollo Theatre in New York City.

Wednesday 27 October 1943
Ella Fitzgerald and the Ink Spots appear at the Silver Screen Canteen in New York City. Duke Ellington and his Orchestra are also featured.

Wednesday 3 November 1943
Ella Fitzgerald records with the Ink Spots for Decca in New York City.
ELLA FITZGERALD, THE INK SPOTS (vocal), JOHN MCGEE (trumpet), BILL DOGGETT (piano), BERNIE MCKAY (guitar), BOB HAGGART (bass), JOHNNY BLOWERS (drums)
Cow Cow Boogie

Friday 5 November 1943
Ella Fitzgerald opens a one-week engagement at the Howard Theatre in Washington, D.C.

Thursday 11 November 1943
Ella Fitzgerald closes at the Howard Theatre in Washington, D.C.

1944

Friday 7 January 1944
Ella Fitzgerald opens a one-week engagement at the Temple Theatre in Rochester, New York. Also on the bill are The Ink Spots, Cootie Williams & his Band and Moke & Poke.

Thursday 13 January 1944
Ella Fitzgerald closes at the Temple Theatre in Rochester, New York.

Tuesday 18 January 1944
While Ella Fitzgerald is on tour with the Ink Spots and Cootie Williams, back in New York the Esquire Award Winners Concert takes place at the Metropolitan Opera House. Ella was voted third in the female vocalist section with 4 votes, behind Billie Holiday (23 votes) and Mildred Bailey (15 votes).

Friday 21 January 1944
Ella Fitzgerald opens a one-week engagement at the Paradise Theatre in Detroit. Also on the bill are The Ink Spots, Cootie Williams & his Band and Moke & Poke.

Thursday 27 January 1944
Ella Fitzgerald closes at the Paradise Theatre in Detroit.

Friday 28 January 1944
Ella Fitzgerald opens a one-week engagement at the Palace Theatre in Cleveland, Ohio. Also on the bill are The Ink Spots, Cootie Williams & his Band and Moke & Poke.

Thursday 3 February 1944
Ella Fitzgerald closes at the Palace Theatre in Cleveland, Ohio.

Friday 4 February 1944

Ella Fitzgerald opens a one-week engagement at the Regal Theatre in Chicago. Also on the bill are The Ink Spots, Cootie Williams & his Band and Moke & Poke.

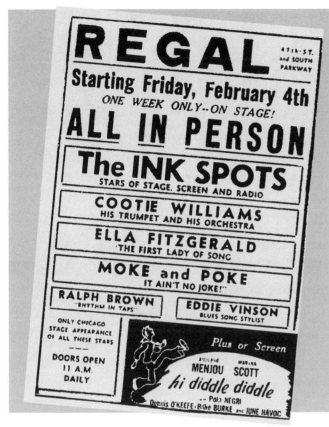

Thursday 10 February 1944

Ella Fitzgerald closes at the Regal Theatre in Chicago.

Friday 18 February 1944

Ella Fitzgerald opens a one-week engagement at the Orpheum Theatre in Minneapolis. Also on the bill are The Ink Spots, Cootie Williams & his Band and Moke & Poke.

Thursday 24 February 1944

Ella Fitzgerald closes at the Orpheum Theatre in Minneapolis.

Ink Spots, Ella And Cootie Keep 'Em Hot

MINNEAPOLIS—Moe Gale is still giving theatre-goers and dance halls the finest attraction traveling today. The attraction composed of Ink Spots, Ella Fitzgerald and Cootie Williams' band is knocking 'em cold everywhere and refusing to be knocked by the cold. For instance the show played here last week and even though the temperature was 12 below, the theatre was packed for each performance while hundreds stood in line outside the theatre defying cold for a chance to see the show. The cast splits next month for a few days with each unit doing single engagements, but will re-unite to complete the 33 weeks later in the month. Cootie Williams will very likely play a dance engagement in Chicago while the split is in vogue.

Friday 25 February 1944

Ella Fitzgerald opens a weekend engagement at the Orpheum Theatre in St. Paul, Minnesota. Also on the bill are The Ink Spots, Cootie Williams & his Band and Moke & Poke.

Monday 28 February 1944

Ella Fitzgerald closes at the Orpheum Theatre in St. Paul, Minnesota.

Wednesday 1 March 1944

Down Beat reviews Ella's latest release:

Ella Fitzgerald
Decca 18586
Cow Cow Boogie / When My Sugar Walks Down The Street
It's good to hear Ella's voice again, even if the material isn't right up her alley. Is she trying to imitate that other Ella, Miss Morse, on *Cow Cow*? Heaven forbid! She used to do considerably better than just all right singing her own style! The *Sugar* side is just that, not quite solid enough to suit most of Ella's oldest and most ardent supporters. Ivie Anderson did a better job on this tune years back! The Ink Spots provide the background on the first, Ella's own mediocre band on the second. Come on, Ella, you can do better than this!

Friday 3 March 1944

Ella Fitzgerald and the Ink Spots/Cootie Williams package open a one-week engagement at the Riverside Theatre in Milwaukee.

Thursday 9 March 1944

Ella Fitzgerald and the Ink Spots/Cootie Williams package close at the Riverside Theatre in Milwaukee, winding up a successful 70-day tour.

Tuesday 21 March 1944

Ella Fitzgerald records with an unknown Orchestra for Decca in New York City (or Chicago?).
ELLA FITZGERALD (vocal)
Once Too Often / Time Alone Will Tell

Tuesday 25 April 1944

Ella Fitzgerald's 26th birthday.
Ella Fitzgerald and the Ink Spots/Cootie Williams package open a one-week engagement at the Orpheum Theatre in Los Angeles.

Monday 1 May 1944

Ella Fitzgerald and the Ink Spots/Cootie Williams package close at the Orpheum Theatre in Los Angeles.
Earlier in the day, Ella and the Cootie Williams Band record transcriptions for AFRS at the NBC Studios in Hollywood.
A-Tisket, A-Tasket / Do Nothin' Till You Hear From Me

Tuesday 9 May 1944
Ella Fitzgerald, The Ink Spots and Cootie Williams & his Band play a one-nighter at the Houston Coliseum in Houston, Texas.

Wednesday 17 May 1944
Ella Fitzgerald, The Ink Spots and Cootie Williams & his Band play for the officers and men at Camp Barksdale in Barksdale Field, Louisiana.

early June 1944
Ella Fitzgerald and the Ink Spots/Cootie Williams package play a one-nighter at the New Post Amphitheatre at Tuskegee Air Field in Tuskegee, Alabama.

Tuesday 13 June 1944
Ella Fitzgerald and the Ink Spots/Cootie Williams package play a one-nighter at the Memorial Hall in Columbus, Ohio.

Friday 16 June 1944
Ella Fitzgerald and the Ink Spots/Cootie Williams package open a one-week engagement at the Stanley Theatre in Pittsburgh.

Thursday 22 June 1944
Ella Fitzgerald and the Ink Spots/Cootie Williams package close at the Stanley Theatre in Pittsburgh.

Friday 23 June 1944
Ella Fitzgerald and the Ink Spots/Cootie Williams package open a one-week engagement at the Earle Theatre in Philadelphia.

Thursday 29 June 1944
Ella Fitzgerald and the Ink Spots/Cootie Williams package close at the Earle Theatre in Philadelphia.

Saturday 1 July 1944
Down Beat reviews Ella's latest release:

ELLA FITZGERALD

Once Too Often
Time Alone Will Tell

Decca 18605

After six straight jazz records, all of them of extraordinary quality, this latest offering by La Fitz falls just a little flat. That's not entirely Ella's fault, however, for her backing could be so much better. There's no need for me to say that this disc will be a big seller, since both tunes are featured in *Pin Up Girl*. Good always on ballads like these, Ella is nevertheless even more effective when working with swing material.

Sunday 30 July 1944
Ella Fitzgerald plays a one-nighter at the Castle Ballroom in St. Louis, Missouri.

Friday 25 August 1944
Ella Fitzgerald opens a one-week engagement at the Apollo Theatre in New York City. Also on the bill are Cootie Williams & his Band and Pigmeat Markham.

Wednesday 30 August 1944
Ella Fitzgerald records with the Ink Spots for Decca in New York City.
Ella Fitzgerald, The Ink Spots (vocal)
Into Each Life Some Rain Must Fall / I'm Making Believe

Thursday 31 August 1944
Ella Fitzgerald closes at the Apollo Theatre in New York City.

Friday 6 October 1944
Ella Fitzgerald, The Ink Spots and Luis Russell & his Band open at the Zanzibar in New York City.

"ORCHIDS TO ELLA FITZGERALD'S INCANDESCENT CHANTING—!"

Back at the New Cafe Zanzibar, clicking solidly, is "the First Lady of Song" Ella Fitzgerald. It was B'way columnist Walter Winchell who sang out with his praise of the Cinderella girl's incandescent chanting on Decca Records which, by the way, should mean a very large bouquet of orchids for our singing star.

The Ink Spots, Dorothy Donegan, Peg Leg Bates and the Berry Brothers share honors with America's No. 1 song stylist at the fabulous New Cafe Zanzibar, a movie director's dream of a nite club.

During the engagement at the Zanzibar, the bass singer in the Ink Spots, Orville 'Hoppy' Jones (42), dies of a cerebral haemmorhage.

Friday 3 November 1944
Ella Fitzgerald attends the funeral at 1pm of Orville 'Hoppy' Jones

Monday 6 November 1944
Ella Fitzgerald records with the Song Spinner and Johnny Long's Orchestra for Decca in New York City.
ELLA FITZGERALD, THE SONG SPINNERS (vocal)
And Her Tears Flowed Like Wine / Confessin'

Thursday 30 November 1944
Ella Fitzgerald closes at the Zanzibar in New York City.

Friday 1 December 1944
Ella Fitzgerald and Jean Parks' Orchestra open a one-week engagement at the Royal Theatre in Baltimore.

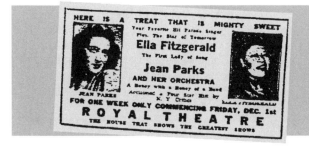

Thursday 7 December 1944
Ella Fitzgerald closes at the Royal Theatre in Baltimore.

Friday 8 December 1944
Ella Fitzgerald opens a one-week engagement at the Howard Theatre in Washington, D.C.

Thursday 14 December 1944
Ella Fitzgerald closes at the Howard Theatre in Washington, D.C.

Friday 29 December 1944
Ella Fitzgerald opens a two-week engagement at the Downtown Theatre in Chicago. Also on the bill are Buck & Bubbles and Ray Kinney's Hawaiian Orchestra.

Basie Angling For Fem Chirp

New York—Count Basie is reported dickering with Ella Fitzgerald to take over the vocal spot which will be left vacant when Thelma Carpenter leaves the band to single at the Ruban Bleu here. Ella's price was an obstacle at presstime and Helen Humes, who sang with the Count more than two years ago, was rumored set to rejoin.

Currently at the Hotel Lincoln on an eight-week return booking, Basie is catching up on record-making at Columbia. Singer Jimmy Rushing is cutting a *Blues* album with a band-from-within-the-band and the full ork is expected to do several wax dates before leaving town. Underway is a plan to cut a *Count Basie Presents* album featuring Benny Goodman, Harry James, Gene Krupa and Frank Sinatra, each artist doing two sides with a small Basie band.

On this third stop at the Lincoln, Basie has the disadvantage of losing late air-time, due to owner Maria Kramer's decision to eliminate wires after 1.00 a.m. because she believes that radio audiences fall off at that hour. Basie leaves the Lincoln February 13 for theater dates, goes into the Roxy in April.

Basie Nixes Ella To Sign New Chirp

New York—Maxine Johnson is the new singer with Count Basie's band at the Hotel Lincoln, replacing Thelma Carpenter, now singing at the Ruban Bleu club here. A deal which would have had Ella Fitzgerald taking over vocals was nixed because the name chirp wanted a piece of the band.

Rumor says that both Lester Young and Jo Jones are coming out of the service but Basie manager Milt Ebbins says it's not true.

Thursday 12 January 1945
Ella Fitzgerald closes at the Downtown Theatre in Chicago.

Monday 26 February 1945
Ella Fitzgerald records with the Ink Spots for Decca in New York City.
ELLA FITZGERALD, THE INK SPOTS (vocal) and studio orchestra
I'm Beginning To See The Light / That's The Way It Is

Wednesday 28 February 1945
Ella Fitzgerald opens a four-week engagement at the Paramount Theatre in New York City. The Ink Spots, Buck& Bubbles and Cootie Williams' Band are also on the bill. The movie presentation is 'Bring On The Girls' starring Veronica Lake, Sonny Tufts, Eddie Bracken and Marjorie Reynolds.

Tuesday 27 March 1945 or Tuesday 13 March

Ella Fitzgerald closes at the Paramount Theatre in New York City.

Tuesday 27 March 1945

Ella Fitzgerald records for Decca in New York City. ELLA FITZGERALD, DELTA RHYTHM BOYS (vocal), RENEE DE KNIGHT (piano), HY WHITE (guitar), HAIG STEPHENS (bass), GEORGE WETTLING (drums)
(It's Only A) Paper Moon / Cry Out Of My Heart (2 takes)

WEDNESDAY 25 APRIL 1945

Ella Fitzgerald's 27th birthday.

Tuesday 1 May 1945

Down Beat reviews Ella's latest Decca release:

ELLA FITZGERALD-INK SPOTS
That's The Way It Is
I'm Beginning To See The Light

Decca 23399

Play the last half of these, Ella's part, and they'll be worth the price. *Beginning* definitely is, even with Bill Kenny's falsetto grating on your nerves. Ella really tears this one apart; she's never done anything quite like it and her vocal is actually thrilling. *That's The Way* follows same pattern, Kenny, Ella and then the entire group on out. This she sings more subdued and it's not quite as fine. *Beginning* is definitely it!

Friday 4 May 1945

Ella Fitzgerald opens a one-week engagement at the Stanley Theatre in Pittsburgh. The Ink Spots and Cootie Williams' Band are also on the bill.

Thursday 10 May 1945

Ella Fitzgerald closes at the Stanley Theatre in Pittsburgh.

Friday 11 May 1945

Ella Fitzgerald opens a one-week engagement at the Earle Theatre in Philadelphia. The Ink Spots and Cootie Williams' Band are also on the bill.

Thursday 17 May 1945

Ella Fitzgerald closes at the Earle Theatre in Philadelphia.

Friday 18 May 1945

Ella Fitzgerald fails to show for the opening of a one-week engagement at the Howard Theatre in Washington, D.C. The Ink Spots and Cootie Williams' Band are also on the bill. Singer Savannah Churchill, who is playing at a local night spot, is contracted to double between the spot and the Howard Theatre.

Saturday 19 May 1945

Ella Fitzgerald arrives in time to do the second show at the Howard Theatre in Washington, D.C. However, A. E. Lichtman, operator of the theatre, is not prepared to countenance Ella's behaviour and cancels her as soon as she arrives.

Friday 1 June 1945

Ella Fitzgerald opens a one-week engagement at the RKO Theatre in Boston. The Ink Spots and Cootie Williams' Band are also on the bill.

Thursday 7 June 1945

Ella Fitzgerald closes at the RKO Theatre in Boston.

RKO, BOSTON

This all-sepia show had a part-sepia audience that went wild and Ella Fitzgerald and the Ink Spots added frenzy to pandemonium… Miss Fitzgerald teams with Bill Kenny for 'Into Each Life Some Rain Must Fall' for more applause dividends. Whole show is torrid entertainment.
VARIETY

Ella Fitzgerald Stands Up Howard Theatre Audience

WASHINGTON

Did Ella Fitzgerald deliberately snub her audience at the Howard Theatre when she failed to appear for an engagement?

This question was asked in the show world when the first lady of swing failed to appear with the crack unit in which she had been playing for 16 weeks in white theatres.

The songstress has been a top feature in a deluxe show including the Ink Spots, Cootie Williams's orchestra. Coke and Poke and Ralph Brown.

Failed to Appear

On opening day, Friday, May 18, Miss Fitzgerald failed to answer the roll call for the first show and according to the Gale office, who handles the star, left for New York after the Earle Theatre date in Philadelphia, instead of coming directly here.

A special announcement by Bill Kenny, of the Ink Spots, at Friday's opening show offered as an excuse the lack of train accommodations and promised her for the next show. Consequently everyone held their seats for two shows.

Lichtman Cracks Down

A. E. Lichtman, operator of the theatre, emphasized the unfavorable word-of-mouth by disgruntled customers on opening day.

Not until the second show Saturday did the singer show up and then after Mr. Lichtman had contacted Savannah Churchill, who agreed to do double duty between the Howard and a local night spot.

Mr. Lichtman gave orders he would not stand for such conduct from any performers, big or little, playing the Howard and stood by his word by cancelling Miss Fitzgerald as soon as she arrived. Lichtman has had to take such drastic steps to penalize a performer since he acquired the Howard a score of years back.

Friday 8 June 1945

Ella Fitzgerald opens a one-week engagement at the Apollo Theatre in New York City. The Ink Spots, Cootie Williams' Band, Coke & Poke and Ralph Brown are also on the bill.

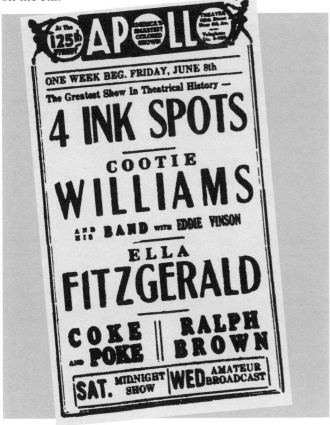

Thursday 14 June 1945

Ella Fitzgerald closes at the Apollo Theatre in New York City.

Friday 15 June 1945

Ella Fitzgerald opens a one-week engagement at the Stanley Theatre in Pittsburgh. The Ink Spots and Cootie Williams' Band are also on the bill.

Thursday 21 June 1945

Ella Fitzgerald closes at the Stanley Theatre in Pittsburgh.

Friday 29 June 1945

Ella Fitzgerald opens a one-week engagement at the Chicago Theatre in Chicago. The Ink Spots and Cootie Williams' Band are also on the bill.

Thursday 5 July 1945

Ella Fitzgerald closes at the Chicago Theatre in Chicago.

Friday 13 July 1945

Ella Fitzgerald opens a one-week engagement at the Orpheum Theatre in Minneapolis. The Ink Spots and Cootie Williams' Band are also on the bill.

Saturday 15 July 1945

Ella and Cootie Williams appear on the cover of *Down Beat*:

Thursday 19 July 1945

Ella Fitzgerald closes at the Orpheum Theatre in Minneapolis.

August 1945

Metronome reviews Ella's latest Decca release:

Ella Fitzgerald–Delta Rhythm Boys

It's Only a Paper Moon A–
Cry You Out of My Heart B–
The teaming of Ella with the tasteful Delta Rhythm group is a vast improvement on her former forced alliance with the Ink Spots. *Paper* is a great example of Ella's consummate ease of style and phrasing. The other side falls short only by the inferiority of the tune. (Decca 23425)

Friday 3 August 1945

Ella Fitzgerald opens a one-week engagement at the Regal Theatre in Chicago. The Ink Spots and Cootie Williams' Band are also on the bill.

Thursday 9 August 1945

Ella Fitzgerald closes at the Regal Theatre in Chicago.

Friday 10 August 1945

Ella Fitzgerald opens a one-week engagement at the Downtown Theatre in Detroit. Also on the bill are Cootie Williams & his Band and the Ink Spots.

Thursday 16 August 1945

Ella Fitzgerald closes at the Downtown Theatre in Detroit. Don Hodges reviews the show for *Metronome*:

COOTIE–ELLA–INK SPOTS
The Mood Was Coot

Downtown Theatre, Detroit

Very few, if any, changes have taken place in the general run of the shows put on by this Big Three Unit, since it was first organized some months ago. There is great improvement in Cootie's leadership, and in Ella's vocal renditions, but the Spots remain the drag of the show.

The band's opener, *Roll 'Em*, brought out Cootie's fine horn and 48 measures of wild tenor by Sam Taylor.

Eddie Vinson, usually a show-stopper, was just a little disappointing with his now too familiar *Red Blues*, followed up by another blues on the very same kick, *Juice Head Baby*. His alto-work is still excitingly good.

Cootie's latest composition, *Mood For Coot*, started out in a definitely macabre vein. The choice of mutes was poor for this particular house's P.A. system, making it only possible for the immediate front rows to hear the sombre strains. As the *Mood* continued it took on a different aspect making this number one of William's best efforts to date. This number with a revamp in harmony and change of mutes might hit the *Do Nothin'* (also a Williams original) mark.

Ella is still tops in her unique song styling, getting things out of her numbers which most chirps would find difficult to do. *Gotta Be This Or That* was right in her groove, and on *Sentimental Journey* she was supported by one of the best backgrounds heard by your writer to date. Though clever, *A-Tisket A-Tasket* is a little time-worn now. As an encore Ella's improvising (à la Jacquet) on *Flying Home* was a sender!

House of Joy, although it's been featured many times before, was the best instrumental that the band put down, spotting 16 and 32 measure solos by almost everyone in the outfit. It's "jam" all the way through *Fish Market* riffs to a *Flying Home* finish!

The band's portion of the program was too limited due to the too large portion allotted to the Ink Spots. There were no Sextet numbers this time. However, the band kicked like mad on the numbers played behind the acts. *Perdido* and *Liza* are two fine examples. Gershwin's tune spotted very interestingly exciting improvising by the pianist. Methinks Cootie and his boys are ready to cut out on their own and leave the Spots to drift alone!!!

Friday 17 August 1945

Ella Fitzgerald opens a one-week engagement at the National Theatre in Louisville, Kentucky. The Ink Spots and Cootie Williams' Band are also on the bill.

Thursday 23 August 1945

Ella Fitzgerald closes at the National Theatre in Louisville, Kentucky.

Wednesday 29 August 1945

Ella Fitzgerald records with Randy Brooks and his Orchestra for Decca in New York City.

ELLA FITZGERALD (vocal), RANDY BROOKS, ERNIE ENGLUND, GEORGE BARDON (trumpets), HARRY BROOKS (trombone), EDDIE CAINE, PAUL BARDON (alto saxes), STUART ANDERSON, JOHN LESKO (tenor saxes), EDDIE SHOMER (baritone sax), SHORTY ALLEN (piano), PAUL LAJOIE (bass), SONNY MANN (drums)

A Kiss Goodnight / Benny's Coming Home On Saturday

Thursday 30 August 1945

Ella Fitzgerald opens a one-week engagement at the Royal Theatre in Baltimore. Also on the bill are Cootie Williams & his Band and the Ink Spots.

Wednesday 5 September 1945

Ella Fitzgerald closes at the Royal Theatre in Baltimore.

Thursday 6 September 1945

Ella Fitzgerald opens a one-week engagement at the Adams Theatre in Newark, New Jersey. Also on the bill are Cootie Williams & his Band and the Ink Spots.

Wednesday 12 September 1945

Ella Fitzgerald closes at the Adams Theatre in Newark, NJ.

Thursday 13 September 1945

Ella Fitzgerald opens a 4-night engagement at the Metropolitan Theatre in Providence, Rhode Island. Also on the bill are Cootie Williams & his Band and the Ink Spots.

Sunday 16 September 1945

Ella Fitzgerald closes at the Metropolitan Theatre in Providence, Rhode Island.

Tuesday 25 September 1945

Ella Fitzgerald guest stars on NBC Radio's Chesterfield Show in New York City.

Thursday 4 October 1945

Ella Fitzgerald records with Vic Schoen and his Orchestra for Decca in New York City.

ELLA FITZGERALD (vocal), RALPH MUSSILO, CHARLES GENDUSO, LOUIS RUGGIERO (trumpets), WILLIAM PRITCHARD (trombone), BENNIE KAUFMAN, SID COOPER (alto saxes), SID RUBIN, HARRY FELDMAN (tenor saxes), MOE WECHSLER (piano), HY WHITE (guitar), FELIX GIOBBE (bass), IRV KLUGER (drums)

Flying Home

Monday 8 October 1945

Ella Fitzgerald records with Louis Jordan and his Tympany Five for Decca in New York City.

ELLA FITZGERALD (vocal), LOUIS JORDAN (alto sax/vocal), AARON IZENHALL (trumpet), JOSH JACKSON (tenor sax), BILL DAVIES (piano), CARL HOGAN (guitar), JESSE SIMPKINS (bass), EDDIE BYRD (drums), HARRY DIAL (maracas), VIC LOURIE (claves)

Stone Cold Dead In De Market / Petootie Pie (2 takes)

Friday 12 October 1945

Ella Fitzgerald records as Ella and her V-Disc Jumpers for V-Discs in New York City.

ELLA FITZGERALD (vocal), CHARLIE SHAVERS (trumpet), LOU McGARITY (trombone), PEANUTS HUCKO (clarinet), AL SEARS (tenor sax), BUDDY WEED (piano), REMO PALMIERI (guitar), TRIGGER ALPERT (bass), BUDDY RICH (drums)

That's Rich / I'll Always Be In Love With You / I'll See You In My Dreams

Wednesday 5 December 1945

Ella Fitzgerald opens an extended engagement at the Zanzibar Club in New York City. The Ink Spots and Cootie Williams' Band are also on the bill.

Thursday 6 December 1945

Ella Fitzgerald is scheduled to make an appearance at the star-studded Page One Ball at Madison Square Garden in New York City. The bands of Duke Ellington, Hal McIntyre, Eddie Condon and Woody Herman are also on the bill.

Monday 10 December 1945

Ella Fitzgerald is the featured guest star on CBS radio's 'Jack Smith Show'.

Big Money For Ella On Radio Stint

Ella Fitzgerald hits another high water mark in her spectacular singing career next Monday night, December 10, when she appears as a featured guest artist on the famous Jack Smith variety show from coast to coast over the Columbia Broadcasting System. The broadcast takes to the air at 7:15 pm.

The "Tisket-a-Tasket" girl will receive the highest figure ever paid to a Negro artist for appearing on the show, which shows conclusively the high esteem in which her talent is held by the officials of the Proctor and Gamble Company, sponsors of the show. She will be paid more than double the fee given to any previous race artist who has occupied a guest spot on the program. Informed radio circles here in New York unofficially place the figure at $1250.

Friday 14 December 1945

Ella Fitzgerald is selected as the "Singing Queen" for the campus queen ball at the Manhattan Center Ballroom. Proceeds go to the National Foundation for Infantile Paralysis.

Monday 17 December 1945

Ella Fitzgerald is guest star on radio's 'Schaefer Star Revue'.

1946

Ella Fitzgerald and the Cootie Williams band continue their successful run at the Café Zanzibar in New York City.

Sunday 13 January 1946

The broadcast from the Zanzibar is reviewed by George Simon for *Metronome*:

COOTIE WILLIAMS
This Fella's For Ella
The Zanzibar, New York. MBS, January 13, 11:45 PM.

Highlight of this show was Ella Fitzgerald, who for my money is so far ahead of all other singers on the air right now that they ought to give her a wavelength all to herself. She did just one tune on this quarter hour sustainer, *Patootie Pie*, a pretty inane vehicle for her, but one with which she did wonders. Not only was her singing absolutely stupendous, but she followed it with some wonderful scatting, as she and Cootie played one of those question and answer games.

Cootie's band was impressive too, with some wonderful bassist with a big, sharp tone and a prodigious beat cutting through handsomely. (He's Cootie's find, Jimmy Glover, eighteen years old and signed to a five term Williams pact— Ed.) The opening *Gee It's Good To Hold You* was handsomely scored with the out-of-tune trumpets not detracting too much and Cootie growling. Open horn would have been more effective on this number. Then came Ella, followed by *Caldonia* with Cootie going great. Wind-up was a one o'clock jumpish thing titled (with great imagination) *Jumpin' at the Zanzibar*, spotting a fine jazz trombone and with that bass cutting through magnificently again.

Friday 18 January 1946

Ella Fitzgerald records with Louis Armstrong and Bob Haggart's Orchestra for Decca in New York City.
ELLA FITZGERALD (vocal), LOUIS ARMSTRONG (trumpet/vocal), BILLY BUTTERFIELD (trumpet), BILL STEGMEYER (clarinet/alto sax), GEORGE KOENIG (alto sax), JACK GREENBERG (tenor sax), ART DRELLINGER (tenor sax), MILTON CHATZ (baritone sax), JOE BUSHKIN (piano), DANNY PERRI (guitar), TRIGGER ALPERT (bass), COZY COLE (drums), BOB HAGGART (conductor) *You You Won't Be Satisfied* (vLA,EF) / *The Frim Fram Sauce* (vLA,EF)

Monday 21 January 1946

Ella Fitzgerald and the Cootie Williams band broadcast on WNEW's 'Let's Go Night Clubbing' from the Café Zanzibar in New York City.
It's Only A Paper Moon / The Honey Dripper

Wednesday 23 January 1946

Ella Fitzgerald appears on CBS radio's 'Jack Smith Show.'

Radio Mark To Ella Fitzgerald

NEW YORK—Ella Fitzgerald scored another smash artistic triumph last Wednesday night when she played a repeat performance as guest star on the famous "Jack Smith Show," heard coast-to-coast nightly over the Columbia Broadcasting System.

Miss Fitzgerald chose this broadcast for the introduction of her novel arrangement of the current pop favorite, "Chickery Chick." Her appearance set a precedent for the program as she was the first artist to play a return engagement within a period of less than six weeks.

Saturday 2 February 1946

Ella Fitzgerald appears at the Amsterdam News Annual Benefit at the Brooklyn Academy of Music.
Also on the bill are Billie Holiday, Dinah Washington, Billy Eckstine, The Ink Spots and Savannah Churchill.

Thursday 21 February 1946

Ella Fitzgerald records for Decca in New York City.
ELLA FITZGERALD (vocal), BILLY KYLE (piano), JIMMY SHIRLEY (guitar), JUNIOR RAGLIN (bass), SYLVESTER PAYNE (drums)
I'm Just A Lucky So-And-So / I Didn't Mean A Word I Said

Thursday 28 February 1946

Ella Fitzgerald and the Cootie Williams band broadcast on WNEW's 'Let's Go Night Clubbing' from the Café Zanzibar in New York City.

Broadway Chatter...
Ella Fitzgerald has been busy during the last few weeks negotiating the purchase of a poultry farm near Freehold, N. J.

Saturday 2 March 1946

Ella Fitzgerald broadcasts of the 'Negro Newspaper Week' program in New York City. She sings *Just A'Sittin' And A'Rockin'*.

Tuesday 5 March 1946

Ella Fitzgerald closes at the Café Zanzibar in New York City.

Thursday 7 March 1946
Ella Fitzgerald opens a two-week engagement at Club 21 in Washington, D.C.

Wednesday 20 March 1946
Ella Fitzgerald closes at Club 21 in Washington, D.C.

Friday 22 March 1946
Ella Fitzgerald opens a one-week engagement at the Royal Theatre in Baltimore.

Thursday 28 March 1946
Ella Fitzgerald closes at the Royal Theatre in Baltimore.

Monday 8 April 1946
Ella Fitzgerald opens a one-week engagement headlining the annual Pine Street YMCA circus at the Opera House, Kiel Auditorium in St. Louis.

Ella Fitzgerald As Queen When She Appears At St. Louis Circus

ST. LOUIS—"At Melody Mansion" is one of the colorful features of the annual Pine Street YMCA circus to be held this week in the great Opera House of Kiel Auditorium, April 8 through 13.

This scene will feature the headliners of the show including Ella Fitzgerald, Dorothy Donegan, the Ink Spots, the Edwards Sisters and Cootie Williams' Orchestra.

This array of stars will be backed by a grand slam of local talent including the Sumner High School Choir, Les Pierrettes, Spotts' Rockettes and Pork and Beans, who will be host and Butler in the colorful grand ballroom of the Dixie Mansion.

The finale "Easter Parade" will be set of "Fifth Avenue" and will feature the entire cast.

Saturday 13 April 1946
Ella Fitzgerald closes at the annual Pine Street YMCA circus at the Opera House, Kiel Auditorium in St. Louis.

Thursday 25 April 1946
Ella Fitzgerald's 28th birthday.

Friday 26 April 1946
Ella Fitzgerald opens a one-week engagement at the Paradise Theatre in Detroit.

Thursday 2 May 1946
Ella Fitzgerald closes at the Paradise Theatre in Detroit.

George Simon reviews Ella's latest release in *Metronome*:

Ella, Now Making Records That Are Stellar, Quite Different from Her Basket That Was Yella
Ella Fitzgerald

I Didn't Mean A Word I Said A–
I'm Just a Lucky So-and-So A–

That these are two great sides in themselves is fine and good. That they herald the approach of a phase of Ella Fitzgerald's career when she will at last be presented as she should be presented on records is even finer and better. For it is not only Ella's great phrasing, her amazing musical conceptions, her ability to make some good out of a song as dull and trite as *I Didn't Mean A Word I Said*, as well as out of a great song like *I'm a Lucky So-and-So*, but it is the overall, relaxed feel of these two sides, with Ella combining her talents with those of Billy Kyle's excellent trio, that revive hope in the revival of this great singer.

Ella likes to sing like this. The simpler the background, the more she can do, the happier she is. Recently she completed an engagement at a New Jersey night club. "I did all the things they wanted me to," she says, "but I really got my kicks late at night when I'd join with the band and just sing licks and sort of become part of the band."

Those of us who knew Ella when she joined Chick Webb's band late in 1935 recall her penchant for being a part of the band. Unable to play an instrument, she'd stand beside the band, singing sax figures, waving her hands along with brass figures, I've always felt she should have been a trumpeter. Ella feels differently. She thinks she should have been a tenorman.

Ella has recorded some of her riffing. She made a sensational V-disc of a thing called *That's Rich*, on which she sings breaks as an eight-piece, all-star group plays *Bugle Blues*. She has recorded the same sort of thing for Decca on *Flyin' Home* and she wishes they'd release it, but so far they haven't seen the light.

Still, Ella is faring better now than she has been for several years. Being tied up with and down to those Ink Spots must have been a horrible drag, musically. She's far too great a singer to be associated with anything like that.

Not that Ella hasn't made fine records in the past, especially things like *Undecided* and *If Dreams Come True* with the Webb band. How Ella still raves about Chick! She is still truly grateful to the late little drummer, grateful for his having discovered her, having featured her, having been so completely unselfish about everything. Ella was his only girl singer; he never wanted one. Even when Bardu Ali, who fronted his band, caught Ella at the Apollo the week Chick was playing the Harlem Opera House, and raved and raved to Chick about her, the little man wouldn't listen. So Bardu just stuck Ella into Chick's dressing-room and when Chick came off stage harnessed guitarist John Trueheart and made Ella sing. Chick broke down and Ella was in.

And now it looks as if maybe Decca is breaking down a little bit, too. First they let Ella sing with Louis Armstrong, and now they're putting her by herself with the right sort of backing. Now, if they'd only release her *Flyin' Home*!

Right: Ella is the cover girl on the May 1946 issue of Metronome.

Friday 31 May 1946

Ella Fitzgerald opens a one-week engagement at the Apollo Theatre in New York City. The Willie Bryant Band, Holmes & Jean, Paul Smith, Maxie Armstrong and George Williams are also on the bill.

The show is reviewed by Leonard Feather for *Metronome*:

ELLA FITZGERALD—WILLIE BRYANT
Ella Scats; Willie Chats
Apollo, New York.

Sharing the billing with Willie Bryant's new band, Ella provided as many vocal thrills as ever. She has gained in poise and personality through the years without losing any of the spontaneity that is such an important part of her charm. The two highlights of her appearance were the delightful Calypso item, *Stone Cold Dead in the Market*, in which she took over Louis Jordan's role on the record and did the whole thing alone in a superbly authentic Trinidad accent, and *Lady Be Good*, notable for a long series of riff-choruses, or scat singing, in which, though there were too many familiar and borrowed licks, Ella's phrasing was entrancingly easy and instrumental.

Willie Bryant emceed the show in his usual flawless manner. Here is one of the most naturally amusing and likeable personalities on any stage. Seeing Willie front a band again brought nostalgic memories, too. Of the group he fronted in the 1930's, which at one time or another included Teddy Wilson, Benny Carter and Ben Webster, Willie only has one original member back, trumpeter Bob Williams. (Willie followed the unusual policy of introducing every man in the band by name, and did it in such a manner that it bored nobody.)

Pianist-arranger Bill Doggett is in musical charge of the unit and was heard in a boogie-woogie solo. Others are Leroy Harris (ex-Hines), playing good alto and singing well on *Lucky So-and-So*; Jimmy Powell (ex-Basie), pouring some Carteresque *Cocktails for Two* out of his alto; Billy Taylor, Jr., son of the noted bassman, and a good bassist himself; trombonists Steve Pullum, Dan Minor and Dickie Wells, the last two both ex-Basie.

They Caged the Canary, It Cost Her 15 Bucks

New York—The cab meter ticked past $10 and the cabby squirmed in his seat. Three hours in front of a building is a long wait. Ella Fitzgerald, the swing canary, had stepped out of the cab three hours earlier saying, "I'll be right out—please wait."

She's gone into the building to sign final papers for a series of radio guest appearances. But that was three hours earlier. Why the delay?

Facts were that Ella, after completing her business, stepped into the elevator to return to the cab and her next show at the Apollo when midway between the 22nd and 21st floor the car stopped. And that caged the canary.

But, the cabby waited and picked up a $5 tip—15 buck total!

Ella missed the show. Would have been cheaper missing the elevator.

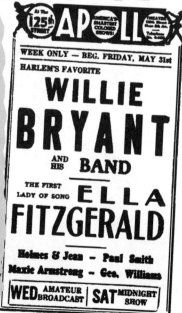

Thursday 6 June 1946

Ella Fitzgerald closes at the Apollo Theatre in New York City.

July 1946

Metronome reviews Ella's latest Decca release:

Ella Fitzgerald-Louis Jordan
Stone Cold Dead In The Market A–
Petootie Pie B

To those who know Ella and Louis well, their satire on a calypso song will seem riotously funny. Both display perfect West Indian accents in an amusing song, with appropriate accompaniment. The other side has some good Fitzgerald in the more customary Yankee vein. (Decca 23546)

Wednesday 10 July 1946

Ella Fitzgerald opens a 9-day engagement at the Riviera Club in St. Louis, Missouri.

Thursday 18 July 1946

Ella Fitzgerald closes at the Riviera Club in St. Louis, Missouri.

Friday 19 July 1946

Ella Fitzgerald opens a one-week engagement at the Regal Theatre in Chicago. Dizzy Gillespie and his Orchestra are also on the bill.

Sunday 21 July 1946

Ella Fitzgerald is presented with the Chicago Defender's 'Queen of Swing' award at the Regal Theatre in Chicago.

Thursday 25 July 1946

Ella Fitzgerald closes at the Regal Theatre in Chicago.

Kentucky Awaits Ella 'Ole Tucky'

NEWPORT, Ky—The staid precincts of Kentucky are in for a pleasant surprise next week when Ella Fitzgerald opens a two-week engagement at the Latin Quarter Club here. Cause for all the excitement will be the Tisket-Tasket girl's rhythmic swing version of "My Old Kentucky Home" a recent addition to her repertoire.

Ella has recently turned her attention to native folk music and nursery rhymes as a source for new music. The first of the old tunes to attract her attention was the familiar tune about the Blue Grass State. She plans to record her swing version of the tune along with several others in a folk album which she hopes to have completed by the fall of 1947.

Saturday 27 July 1946
Ella Fitzgerald opens a 12-night engagement in Virginia Beach.

Wednesday 7 August 1946
Ella Fitzgerald closes in Virginia Beach.

Friday 16 August 1946
Ella Fitzgerald opens a two-week engagement at the Coronet Club in Philadelphia opposite the Tiny Bradshaw Orchestra.

Gay Crowd of First-Nighters Gives Ella Clamorous Reception

Ella Fitzgerald, America's first lady of swing, scored one of the most spectacular hits of her career last Friday night as the headliner of the new show at the Coronet Club.

A brilliant crowd of headliners in the fields of sports, politics and the entertainment world gave the winsome songstress one of the most tumultous receptions in Quaker City history.

Tiny Bradshaw's band, co-stars of the fast moving show, brought down the house also with their bouncy rhythms interspersed with the redhead's dynamic vocals.

Son and Sonny, playing their first local night club engagement, impr...

The initial show headlined by Cootie Williams's orchestra did a gross of $23,000 for two weeks, topping any similar take for a similar period in a black and tan club in the history of the Quaker City.

Thursday 29 August 1946
Ella Fitzgerald records for Decca in New York City.
ELLA FITZGERALD, DELTA RHYTHM BOYS (vocal), RENEE DE KNIGHT (piano), JIMMY SHIRLEY (guitar), LAMONT MOTEN (bass), EDDIE BOURNE (drums)
For Sentimental Reasons / It's A Pity To Say Goodnight
In the evening she closes at the Coronet Club in Philadelphia.

Friday 30 August 1946
Ella Fitzgerald opens a one-week engagement at the Earle Theatre in Philadelphia.

Thursday 5 September 1946
Ella Fitzgerald closes at the Earle Theatre in Philadelphia.

Friday 13 September 1946
Ella Fitzgerald opens a one-week engagement at the Apollo Theatre in New York City. Cootie Williams and his Band, The Vagabonds and Spider Bruce are also on the bill.

Ella Fitzgerald (above) and Cootie (left) on stage at the Apollo.

**FITZGERALD—WILLIAMS
vocal jam best that am**
Apollo, New York.

Until Queen Ella walked onto this stage, this was just another good Apollo show. After she had finished, the packed house was in an uproar and could have sat through at least an hour or more of her sensational singing, easy stage presence and continual good humor. The buxom gal is unquestionably the greatest singer of them all today, as this show gave further and unnecessary evidence. She began with a groovy *Route 66*, marred only by a hoked up bit of business about "I forgot the words…", slid easily into *I Don't Know Why*, done in beautiful style, and then the successful bit that she waxed for Decca, *Patootie Pie*. Benny Goodman told Simon that he listens to this disc every morning and it's easy to dig why, since *Pie* is Ella's meat. The piece de resistance was, of course, Ella's now-famous vocal jam session on *Lady Be Good* and good for at least 6 sensational choruses. She has some set riffs now that would make many top musicians' eyes bug out and also offers a quick imitation of Slam Stewart that is good for laughs. The whole thing packs more wallop than any music business specialty to be heard around today. Needless to say, this broke it up and The Queen had to come back for the obvious *Stone Cold Dead*. She left them screaming for more and could have sung the rest of the night out for them and us too.

Cootie Williams was as impressive as usual up front, but the support of his band left something to be desired. The Coot is evidently on a Hampton kick with tenor sax battles, forced comedy antics and plenty of screamers, but at least they kick and the saxes sounded good and in tune. Best number was a subdued, muted clarinet, trombone and trumpet opus called *Mood for Coot* that was obviously inspired by something of The Duke's. Cootie sang too (on *Let's Do The Whole Thing*) in a gravel-voiced Armstrong vein and not bad either. His horn, of course, was great and probably the very closest thing around to The King.

Broadway Chatter…
Ella Fitzgerald is inviting all members of the theatrical profession to join in a fund raising campaign to aid the families of lynch victims.

Thursday 19 September 1946
Ella Fitzgerald closes at the Apollo Theatre in New York City.

Friday 27 September 1946
Ella Fitzgerald opens a one-week engagement at the Paradise Theatre in Detroit. Dizzy Gillespie and his Orchestra are also on the bill.

Thursday 3 October 1946
Ella Fitzgerald closes at the Paradise Theatre in Detroit.

Friday 4 October 1946
Ella Fitzgerald opens a two-week engagement at Club 845 in the Bronx, New York.

Thursday 17 October 1946
Ella Fitzgerald closes at Club 845 in the Bronx, New York.

Friday 18 October 1946
Ella Fitzgerald opens a one-week engagement at the Howard Theatre in Washington, D.C. Dizzy Gillespie and his Orchestra and Cozy Cole with dancers from 'Carmen Jones' are also on the bill.

Thursday 24 October 1946
Ella Fitzgerald closes at the Howard Theatre in Washington, D.C.

Friday 25 October 1946
Ella Fitzgerald opens a one-week engagement at the Royal Theatre in Baltimore. Dizzy Gillespie and his Orchestra and Cozy Cole with dancers from 'Carmen Jones' are also on the bill.

Thursday 31 October 1946
Ella Fitzgerald closes at the Royal Theatre in Baltimore.

Friday 1 November 1946

Dizzy Gillespie and his Orchestra and Ella Fitzgerald play a one-nighter at the Palais Royal Casino in Norfolk, Virginia.

Monday 4 November 1946

Dizzy Gillespie and his Orchestra and Ella Fitzgerald open a two-night engagement at the Booker T Theatre in Norfolk, Virginia.

Tuesday 5 November 1946

Dizzy Gillespie and his Orchestra and Ella Fitzgerald close at the Booker T Theatre in Norfolk, Virginia.

Sunday 17 November 1946

Ella Fitzgerald and the Dizzy Gillespie Orchestra play a dance at the Savoy Ballroom in Chicago.

Tuesday 10 December 1946

Ella Fitzgerald and the Dizzy Gillespie Orchestra play a one-nighter at the Dorie Miller Auditorium in Austin, Texas.

Ella Fitzgerald Unveils Plaque Given By Her to Honor U.S. Hero

AUSTIN, Tex—Ella Fitzgerald interrupted her swing music activities during her visit here Tuesday to pay a lasting tribute to the memory of America's great Naval hero, Dorie Miller.

Here to play a dance date at the auditorium, named after the World War II immortal, Miss Fitzgerald presented a plaque, as a gift from the singer, to be prominently displayed in the hall.

The plaque will be mounted when it arrives early in January. Finishing touches on the casting are being completed in New York.

The presentation ceremonies were made in absentia (of the plaque, that is) because Miss Fitzgerald will be filling an engagement in the Gotham area during January.

Wednesday 11 December 1946

Ella Fitzgerald and the Dizzy Gillespie Orchestra play a one-nighter in Houston, Texas.

Thursday 12 December 1946

Ella Fitzgerald and the Dizzy Gillespie Orchestra open a two-nighter in San Antonio, Texas.

Friday 13 December 1946

Ella Fitzgerald and the Dizzy Gillespie Orchestra close in San Antonio, Texas.

Saturday 14 December 1946

Ella Fitzgerald and the Dizzy Gillespie Orchestra play a one-nighter in Austin, Texas.

Sunday 15 December 1946

Ella Fitzgerald and the Dizzy Gillespie Orchestra play a one-nighter in San Antonio, Texas.

Tuesday 17 December 1946

Ella Fitzgerald and the Dizzy Gillespie Orchestra play a one-nighter in Little Rock, Arkansas.

Wednesday 18 December 1946

Ella Fitzgerald and the Dizzy Gillespie Orchestra play a one-nighter in Ruston, Louisiana.

Thursday 19 December 1946

Ella Fitzgerald and the Dizzy Gillespie Orchestra play a one-nighter in Galveston, Texas.

Friday 20 December 1946

Ella Fitzgerald and the Dizzy Gillespie Orchestra play a one-nighter in Alexandria, Louisiana.

Wednesday 25 December 1946

Ella Fitzgerald and the Dizzy Gillespie Orchestra play a one-nighter in Jackson, Mississippi.

Thursday 26 December 1946

Ella Fitzgerald and the Dizzy Gillespie Orchestra play a one-nighter in Memphis, Tennessee.

Friday 27 December 1946

Ella Fitzgerald and the Dizzy Gillespie Orchestra play a one-nighter in Birmingham, Alabama.

Saturday 28 December 1946

Ella Fitzgerald and the Dizzy Gillespie Orchestra play a one-nighter in Nashville, Tennessee.

Monday 30 December 1946

Ella Fitzgerald and the Dizzy Gillespie Orchestra play a one-nighter in Atlanta, Georgia.

Tuesday 31 December 1946

Ella Fitzgerald and the Dizzy Gillespie Orchestra play a one-nighter in Meridian, Mississippi.

1947

Wednesday 1 January 1947

Ella Fitzgerald and the Dizzy Gillespie Orchestra play a one-nighter in New Orleans.

Thursday 2 January 1947

Ella Fitzgerald and the Dizzy Gillespie Orchestra play a one-nighter in Gulfport, Mississippi.

Friday 3 January 1947

Ella Fitzgerald and the Dizzy Gillespie Orchestra play a one-nighter in Pensacola, Florida.

Saturday 4 January 1947

Ella Fitzgerald and the Dizzy Gillespie Orchestra play a one-nighter in Tuskegee, Alabama.
During the tour, Ella becomes romantically involved with the Gillespie bassist Ray Brown.

Friday 24 January 1947

Ella Fitzgerald records with the Eddie Heywood Orchestra for Decca in New York City.
ELLA FITZGERALD (vocal), LEONARD GRAHAM (trumpet), AL KING (trombone), JIMMY POWELL (alto sax), EDDIE HEYWOOD (piano), BILLY TAYLOR (bass), WILLIAM 'KEG' PURNELL (drums)
Guilty / Sentimental Journey

Sunday 26 January 1947

Ella Fitzgerald opens a one-week engagement at the New Music Hall in Washington, D.C.

Saturday 1 February 1947

Ella Fitzgerald closes at the New Music Hall in Washington, D.C.

Ella To Regale Broadway With "Stone Cold Dead"

NEW YORK—When Ella Fitzgerald's Broadway engagement at the Paramount gets underway next Wednesday the audiences on the great white way will hear and see a dramatically new "production" of her famous Calypso ditty, "Stone Cold Dead in the Market."

Her rendition will highlight a widely diversified group of songs identified with Miss Fitzgerald over the years.

When the recording of Wilmouth Houdini's tragic folk ballad swept the country, Miss Fitzgerald teamed with Louis Jordan vocally, and his small band was used for the music background.

Believing that it had even greater possibilities, she has created a more elaborate arrangement for a large musical aggregation. Cootie Wiliams's band will be the first to present this new version during the engagement at Broadway's top vaudeville house.

Wednesday 5 February 1947

Ella Fitzgerald, the Ink Spots, Cootie Williams' Orchestra, Tip, Tap & Toe and Stump & Stumpy open at the Paramount Theatre in New York City. The movie presentation is 'Easy Come, Easy Go' starring Barry Fitzgerald, Diana Lynn and Sonny Tufts.

Tuesday 11 February 1947

Ella Fitzgerald appears at the Amsterdam News' 8th Annual Brooklyn Benefit at Loew's Bedford Theatre in Brooklyn, New York. Billie Holiday and the Cootie Williams Orchestra are also present.

Wednesday 19 February 1947

Ella Fitzgerald appears at a Housing Dance at the Savoy Ballroom in New York City. Also on the bill are Cootie Williams and his Orchestra, the Ink Spots, Thelma Carpenter, Stump & Stumpy and Tip, Tap & Toe.

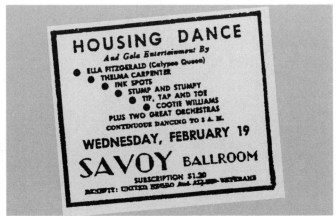

Saturday 22 February 1947
Ella Fitzgerald broadcasts on WOR's 25th Anniversary Show with Tommy Dorsey's Orchestra in New York City.
Guilty

Tuesday 25 February 1947
Ella Fitzgerald, the Ink Spots and Cootie Williams' Orchestra close at the Paramount Theatre in New York City.

Ella Fitzgerald At Carnegie Hall To Headline Monster All-Star Show

A red letter day in swingdom comes up at Carnegie Hall Saturday, March 15 when virtually every top negro name in the popular music field will appear in a gala all star concert at the famous Carnegie Hall. Headlining the galaxy of super stars scheduled to appear will be Ella Fitzgerald, queen of the song stylists. Miss Fitzgerald, who has walked off with virtually every singing poll in the country during the past year has just added the annual Pittsburgh Courier poll to her list of conquests. She was adjudged the best popular singer by a diversified jury of nationally famous personalities, headed by heavyweight champ Joe Louis.

The Carnegie Hall concert promises to be the most exciting music event of the season. The conclave of popular music greats will include top band leaders, ace instrumentalists and the pick of the country's vocalists and novelty units. The projected concert has aroused more interest than any similar popular music event to date. Already the great concert is more than half sold which means an SRO audience will thrill to the performances of the "Tisket-Tasket" girl and the host of other swing greats who will appear.

Saturday 15 March 1947
Ella Fitzgerald is among the guests at a Lionel Hampton Concert (11.30pm) at Carnegie Hall in New York City. Other guests include Dizzy Gillespie, Count Basie, the Ink Spots, Billy Eckstine and Cootie Williams.

Wednesday 19 March 1947
Ella Fitzgerald records with Bob Haggart's Orchestra for Decca in New York City.
ELLA FITZGERALD (vocal), ANDY FERRETTI, CHRIS GRIFFIN, BOB PECK (trumpets), WILL BRADLEY, JACK SATTERFIELD, FREDDIE OHMS (trombones), ERNIE CACERES (baritone sax), STAN FREEMAN (piano), DANNY PERRI (guitar), BOB HAGGART (bass), MOREY FELD (drums), ANDY LOVE QUINTET (vocal group)
A Sunday Kind Of Love (vEF, ALQ) / *That's My Desire* (vEF, ALQ) / *Oh, Lady Be Good* (vEF)

Friday 21 March 1947
Ella Fitzgerald opens a one-week engagement at the Apollo Theatre in New York City. Cootie Williams and his Band, Eddie Rector, the 3 Riffs and Brookins & Van are also on the bill.

Saturday 22 March 1947
Ella Fitzgerald appears on WNEW's 'Saturday Night Swing Session' with Dizzy Gillespie and Count Basie.

Thursday 27 March 1947
Ella Fitzgerald closes at the Apollo Theatre in New York City.

Fire Destroys Ella's Little Yellow Basket

NEW YORK—Ella Fitzgerald, the swing singer deluxe is a very unhappy girl these days and with good reason. The little brown and yellow basket which an admirer presented to her in connection with her "tisket-a-tasket" swing classic several years ago has been lost. A careless visitor to her home last week accidentally dropped a lighted cigarette into it and before anything could be done about it the cherished memento had been consumed.

Saturday 5 April 1947
Ella Fitzgerald broadcasts on WNEW's Saturday Night Swing Session in New York City.
ELLA FITZGERALD, BUDDY RICH (vocal), ROY ROSS (accordion), NICK TAGG (piano), SID CATLETT (drums)
Budella

Thursday 24 April 1947
Ella Fitzgerald opens an engagement at Ye Old Tavern in West Brookfield, Massachusetts.

Friday 25 April 1947
Ella Fitzgerald's 29th birthday.

Wednesday 30 April 1947
Ella Fitzgerald closes at Ye Old Tavern in West Brookfield, Massachusetts.

Friday 2 May 1947

Ella Fitzgerald opens a one-week engagement at the Regal Theatre in Chicago. Cootie Williams & his Band and the Illinois Jacquet Group are also on the bill.

Thursday 8 May 1947

Ella Fitzgerald closes at the Regal Theatre in Chicago.

Friday 9 May 1947

Ella Fitzgerald opens a three-week engagement at Club Bali in Washington, D.C.

Wednesday 21 May 1947

Down Beat reviews Ella's latest Decca release:

Ella Fitzgerald
*** *A Sunday Kind of Love*
**** *That's My Desire*

Anyone who can listen to these two sides and not start revising up any estimates he may have had of Miss Fitzgerald's all-around singing ability, is voice-deaf. First is heart-felt ballad singing, second moves into rhythm singing, backed by the Andy Love quintet, copying the defunct Mel Torme Meltones. (*Decca 23866*)

Thursday 29 May 1947

Ella Fitzgerald closes at Club Bali in Washington, D.C.

Theatre Authority To Back Ella Fitzgerald

NEW YORK—Led by Alan Corelli, important head of the New York Theatre authority, all show business including performers, managers and booking agencies cheering songstress Ella Fitzgerald for her constructive suggestion that an accrediting agency be set up on a national scale to pass upon the worthiness of charity and benefit performances by performers.

Corelli, staunch champion of equal rights, has long been a foe of unscrupulous "benefit" promoters here. As it is today, no permission for the use of artists is granted until the theatre authority has satisfied itself as to the legitimacy of the benefiting cause. The theatre authority and its work inspired Miss Fitzgerald to make her recommendation that the same policy should be enlarged to work on a national scale with some national authority passing on the worth of efforts in which promoters seek to use established artists at no fees.

Friday 13 June 1947

Ella Fitzgerald opens a two-week engagement at the Downbeat Club on 52nd Street in New York City. The club is newly reopened by Louis Shanowitz after its enforced closure only two month previously. Her backing trio is led by Ray Tunia.

New York's 52nd Street Blooms Ella Fitzgerald's Return Plays Part

NEW YORK—Ella Fitzgerald, America's "First Lady of Swing," was the central figure in one of the most exciting night club openings in years when she bowed in as headliner at the famous Downbeat Club on 52nd St. here Friday night. A jam-packed audience of Broadway and Harlem celebrities greeted the beloved sweetheart of song.

Ella is playing a limited two weeks' engagement at the Swing Street bistro. Arrangements have been completed for a coast-to-coast mutual network wire for nightly broadcasts from the club. These airings will begin during the second week of the 'A-tisket A-tasket' girl's stand.

The engagement of Miss Fitzgerald is the first step in a determined campaign by the operators along Gotham's famous swing alley to restore 52nd st. to its former place of importance in the local entertainment and night club picture.

Ella Does Record $7,683 at 'Beat

NEW YORK—Fifty Second Street, mourned by many swing music addicts as being "on the way out," came to life with a vengeance during last week when Ella Fitzgerald did a record smashing $7,683 gross take at the re-opened Downbeat Club.

The Tisket-Tasket girl probably would be held on indefinitely but the fact she is already committed to begin a one-month engagement at the Surf Club in Wildwood, N. J., June 26.

Wednesday 25 June 1947

Ella Fitzgerald closes at the Downbeat Club on 52nd Street in New York City.

Thursday 26 June 1947

Ella Fitzgerald opens a four-week engagement at the Surf Club in Wildwood, New Jersey.

Wednesday 2 July 1947

Down Beat reviews Ella's latest Decca release:

Ella Fitzgerald
***** *Lady Be Good*
*** *Flyin' Home*

You saw right—*Good* drags down five notes—the first time this column has ever fallen on its face so profoundly in the presence of a superior performance. Not content with having consistently made some of the best ballad and novelty records of the past three years, Miss Fitzgerald comes on with two quasi-scat sides which will be listened to just as avidly ten years from now as they are today. Despite clumsy big band backing from Vic Schoen, Ella takes off on the initial chorus and builds to a magnificent climax. Not only is her intonation perfect, her instrumental conception magnificent, the rhythmic effect climactic, but she tosses in some sly digs at Dizzy, Babs, Slam, Hamp, Leo Watson and others by singing variations on some of their better known ideas— at this tempo a sense of humor yet! When you remember the raw youngster who sang with Chick Webb over a decade ago, and think how much she has improved to turn out polished material like this, you can respect not only her ability but that of the little drummer-leader who found her. Despite the wild effect on both these sides, they are well-knit, carefully thought-out musical performances. Brass sections for example might study the way she rides one note on *Home* and keeps the beat swinging all the time she does it.

Tersely, on this one, Ella's a hella. (*Decca 23956*)

Wednesday 11 July 1947

Ella Fitzgerald records with Bob Haggart's Orchestra (personnel unknown) for Decca in New York City.
You're Breaking In A New Heart
Phil Schaap maintains that more of this session survives on 4 acetates in the Decca vaults.

Tuesday 22 July 1947

Ella Fitzgerald records with Bob Haggart's Orchestra for Decca in New York City.
ELLA FITZGERALD (vocal), ANDY FERRETTI (trumpet), WILL BRADLEY, BILLY RAUCH, SEYMOUR SCHAFFER, FREDDIE OHMS (trombones), ART DRELLINGER (clarinet), TOOTS MONDELLO (alto sax), HYMIE SHERTZER (tenor sax), STAN FREEMAN (piano), DANNY PERRI (guitar), BOB HAGGART (bass), NORRIS SHAWKER (drums)
Don't You Think I Oughta Know? / You're Breaking In A New Heart
Ella closes at the Surf Club in Wildwood, New Jersey.

Wednesday 23 July 1947

Ella Fitzgerald opens a four-night engagement at the Sky Club of the Brant Inn in Burlington, Ontario.

Ella Fitzgerald Goes North of the Border

BURLINGTON, Ont—Ella Fitzgerald, "first lady of swing," makes her initial visit to the dominion, July 23, to play a brief engagement at Brant Inn here, a rendezvous built in the shape of a ship and located on Lake Ontario.

Saturday 26 July 1947

Ella closes at the Brant Inn in Burlington, Ontario.

Friday 1 August 1947

Ella Fitzgerald opens a one-week engagement at the Howard Theatre in Washington, D.C. Cootie Williams and his Orchestra are also on the bill.

Tuesday 5 August 1947

Ella Fitzgerald and the Cootie Williams Orchestra broadcast from the Howard Theatre in Washington, D.C.
Oh, Lady Be Good / Across The Alley From The Alamo

Thursday 7 August 1947

Ella Fitzgerald closes at the Howard Theatre in Washington, D.C.

Thursday 14 August 1947

Ella Fitzgerald opens a two-week engagement at the Chanticleer in Baltimore.

Wednesday 27 August 1947

Ella Fitzgerald closes at the Chanticleer in Baltimore.

Thursday 28 August 1947

Ella Fitzgerald guests with Dizzy Gillespie on his closing night at the Downbeat Club on 52nd Street in New York City.

Dizzy Gillespie (right) is entranced as Ella sings with his band at the Downbeat Club on 52nd Street. Ella's boyfriend, bassist Ray Brown, can be seen at the left.

Friday 29 August 1947

Ella Fitzgerald opens a five-week engagement at the Downbeat Club on 52nd Street in New York City.

First Lady Returns to Swing Alley Club

NEW YORK—Ella Fitzgerald will return to Swing Alley on August 29 for a five-week stay at Club Downbeat.

The last time she appeared at the Swing Spot, the management wanted her to stay on for another month, but a long list of commitments forced her to turn down the request.

Meanwhile, jazz musicians are crediting Miss Fitzgerald with the sudden revived interest in jump music. Her hit Decca recording of "Oh Lady be Good" has caused rival record companies to draw on their best jazz talent to make similar waxings.

September 1947

Metronome reviews Ella's latest Decca release:

Ella Fitzgerald

Oh, Lady Be Good A–
Flying Home A–

The high ratings are more for the scatting skill of The First Lady of Jazz than for her choice of riffs and runs. The excursions into Slam Stewartiana, *Dardanella*, *A-tisket A-tasket*, etc. do not represent Ella at her improvising best; but the ease with which she throws off the vocal breaks, her astonishing drive and complete command of her resources do. Backing on the first is by Bob Haggart, second by Vic Schoen, both studio bands held down to rhythmic support and basic chords. (Decca 23956)

Monday 29 September 1947

Ella Fitzgerald guest stars with Dizzy Gillespie Big Band in a concert at Carnegie Hall in New York City. Charlie Parker appears as a guest star.

ELLA FITZGERALD (vocal), DIZZY GILLESPIE, DAVE BURNS, ELMON WRIGHT, RAY ORR, MATTHEW MCKAY (trumpets), TASWELL BAIRD, BILL SHEPHERD (trombones), HOWARD JOHNSON, JOHN BROWN (alto sax), JAMES MOODY, JOE GAYLES (tenor sax), CECIL PAYNE (baritone sax), JOHN LEWIS (piano), MILT JACKSON (vibes), AL MCKIBBON (bass), JOE HARRIS (drums) ELLA FITZGERALD (vocals); HANK JONES (piano) plus Dizzy Gillespie Orchestra:

Almost Like Being In Love (vEF) / *Stairway To The Stars* (vEF) / *Lover Man* (vEF) / *Flyin' Home* (vEF) / *Oh, Lady Be Good* (vEF) / *How High The Moon* (vEF)

Dizzy, Bird, Ella Pack Carnegie

Despite Bad Acoustics, Gillespie Concert Offers Some Excellent Music

By MICHAEL LEVIN

New York—A sell-out crowd in huge Carnegie Hall heard the Dizzy Gillespie band aided by Charlie Parker plus vocal star Ella Fitzgerald run through 120 minutes of largely excellent music. Stand outs of the concert were George Russell's Cubano Bop, directed by the writer, John Lewis' Toccata For Trumpet, and Parker's altoing with the Quintet on numbers he and Gillespie recorded several years ago for Guild.

Miss Fitzgerald, on for the last part of the concert, showed to advantage in a white tailored dinner gown, running through a superb *Stairway To The Stars* and giving Dizzy considerable competition on some chase choruses of *How High The Moon*.

Principal fault of the concert was the acoustic balance. Promoter and commentator Leonard Feather who split the profits with Gillespie could have profited from the Granz concert in the same hall 18 hours earlier.

Granz placed the band mid-stage, and did not use the Carnegie Hall public address system with its speakers placed at the top of the arch. Instead, the band's vocalist and reedmen were heard through two speakers placed on each side of the stage.

Result of using the Hall speakers, placed at the acoustical peak point, was to give the same old barrel effect which has troubled other jazz concerts in the past.

Far left: Ella on satge at Carnegie Hall with Dizzy Gillespie and his Orchestra.

Wednesday 8 October 1947
Ella Fitzgerald closes at the Downbeat Club on 52nd Street in New York City.

Thursday 9 October 1947
Ella Fitzgerald opens a one-week engagement at the Adams Theatre in Newark, New Jersey. Dizzy Gillespie and his Orchestra are also on the bill.

Wednesday 15 October 1947
Ella Fitzgerald closes at the Adams Theatre in Newark, New Jersey.

Thursday 16 October 1947
Ella Fitzgerald opens a one-week engagement at the RKO Theatre in Boston.

Wednesday 22 October 1947
Ella Fitzgerald closes at the RKO Theatre in Boston.

Friday 24 October 1947
Ella Fitzgerald opens a one-week engagement at the Apollo Theatre in New York City. Also on the bill are Buck & Bubbles, Cat Anderson and his Band, Dee Dee Brown and the Ladd Lyon Trio.

Thursday 30 October 1947
Ella Fitzgerald closes at the Apollo Theatre in New York City.

Friday 31 October 1947
Ella Fitzgerald opens a two-week engagement at Club Bali in Washington, D.C.

Thursday 13 November 1947
Ella Fitzgerald closes at Club Bali in Washington, D.C.

Friday 14 November 1947
Ella Fitzgerald opens a one-week engagement at the Paradise Theatre in Detroit. Dizzy Gillespie and his Orchestra are also on the bill.

Thursday 20 November 1947
Ella Fitzgerald closes at the Paradise Theatre in Detroit.

Friday 21 November 1947
Ella Fitzgerald opens a one-week engagement at the Regal Theatre in Chicago. Jimmie Lunceford & his Orchestra and the Illinois Jacquet Group are also on the bill. Ella's trio is Hank Jones (piano), Ray Brown (bass), Charlie Smith (drums).

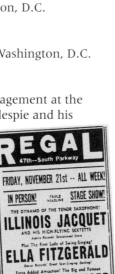

Tuesday 25 November 1947
Ella Fitzgerald broadcasts on the 'Dave Garroway Show' in Chicago.

Thursday 27 November 1947
Ella Fitzgerald closes at the Regal Theatre in Chicago.

Monday 1 December 194
Ella Fitzgerald and her trio (Hank Jones, Ray Brown & Charlie Smith) open a two-week engagement at the Merry-Go-Round nightclub in Youngstown, Ohio.

Wednesday 10 December 1947
Ella Fitzgerald and Ray Brown are married in Youngstown, Ohio.

Ella Is Bride

New York—Ella Fitzgerald, famed jazz singer, was married December 10 to Ray Brown, star bassman recently with Norman Granz and formerly in the Dizzy Gillespie band.

Sunday 14 December 1947
Ella Fitzgerald and her trio close at the Merry-Go-Round nightclub in Youngstown, Ohio.

Thursday 18 December 1947
Ella Fitzgerald records with the Day Dreamers and a small group for Decca in New York City.
ELLA FITZGERALD, THE DAY DREAMERS (vocal)
I Want To Learn About Love / That Old Feeling

Saturday 20 December 1947
Ella Fitzgerald records with a small group for Decca in New York City.
ELLA FITZGERALD (vocal), LEONARD GRAHAM [IDRIES SULIEMAN] (trumpet), HANK JONES (piano), RAY BROWN (bass), CHARLIE SMITH (drums), and others
My Baby Likes To Re-Bop / No Sense / How High The Moon

Tuesday 23 December 1947
Ella Fitzgerald records with a small group for Decca in New York City.
ELLA FITZGERALD (vocal), ILLINOIS JACQUET (tenor sax), SIR CHARLES THOMPSON (organ), HANK JONES (piano), HY WHITE (guitar), JOHN SIMMONS (bass), J. C. HEARD (drums)
I've Got A Feeling I'm Falling / You Turned The Tables On Me / I Cried And Cried And Cried / Robbins Nest

Thursday 25 December 1947
Ella Fitzgerald opens a one-week engagement at the Royal Theatre in Baltimore.

Wednesday 31 December 1947
Ella Fitzgerald closes at the Royal Theatre in Baltimore.

1948

Monday 12 January 1948

Ella Fitzgerald broadcasts on 'Patterns in Melody' in New York City.

Friday 16 January 1948

Ella Fitzgerald and the Illinois Jacquet Group play a concert (8.30pm) at the Bushnell Memorial Auditorium in Hartford, Connecticut.

Ella Fitzgerald And Illinois Jacquet In A Carnegie Concert

Carnegie Hall's staid rafters will sing Saturday night, Jan. 17th, as Ernest Anderson presents Illinois Jacquet and his orchestra along with the First Lady of Swing, Ella (A Tisket A Tasket) Fitzgerald, as the attractions of the Fred Robbins One Nite Stand at 11.30 p.m.

Illinois, the sensational saxophonist, will feature Sir Charles Thompson at the piano, Shadow Wilson at the drums, Al Lucas, bass, Leo Parker, baritone, Joe Newman and Russell Jacquet at the trumpets and J. J. Johnson at the trombone.

Miss Fitzgerald will sing the various songs she made famous as well as new compositions that promise to be the hits of tomorrow.

Both Robbins and Anderson believe Ella and Illinois's combinations of talents will prove one of the biggest musical treats of the New Year.

Saturday 17 January 1948

Ella Fitzgerald and the Illinois Jacquet Group play an afternoon concert at the Town Hall in Philadelphia.
Ella Fitzgerald and the Illinois Jacquet Group play a Fred Robbins One-Nite Stand concert (11.30pm) at Carnegie Hall in New York City.

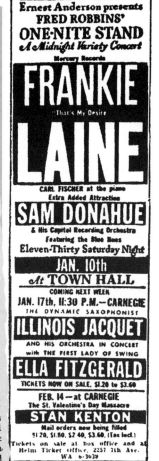

Illinois-Ella Show Draws

New York—The Ella Fitzgerald-Illinois Jacquet unit launched its concert tour with a tremendous wallop at Carnegie Hall, Saturday night January 17.

Despite the third heavy snowfall in a three-week period, a capacity crowd turned out for the Ernie Anderson promotion. Beside selling out the house, 200 onstage seats were sold.

The Carnegie turnout proved a great hypo for the Anderson Saturday-midnight series which had been an off-and-on thing until the preceding week when Frankie Laine and Sam Donahue jammed Town Hall. The latter, of course, doesn't compare with the huge Carnegie in capacity, however.

Premium Prices

With tickets going at a $4.80 top, the box office reaped a few dollars less than $7,500. On-stage chairs went for $6 per.

Even without a better break in the weather, tradesters were of the opinion the attraction easily could have done two capacity nights.

The same combo has sold out on other tour dates; notably Philadelphia, same afternoon as the New York show; Boston, and Detroit. Ticket supply for the latter, staged in conjunction with Jack the Bellboy, was exhausted several days before the date.

Sunday 18 January 1948

Ella Fitzgerald and the Illinois Jacquet Group play an afternoon concert (3.00pm) at Rhodes-On-The-Pawtuxet in Rhodes Place, Providence, Rhode Island.
In the evening they play a concert (8.30pm) at Symphony Hall in Boston, Massachusetts.

Monday 19 January 1948

Ella Fitzgerald and the Illinois Jacquet Group play a concert at the Auditorium in Worcester, Massachusetts.

Tuesday 20 January 1948

Ella Fitzgerald and the Illinois Jacquet Group play a concert in New Haven, Connecticut.

Thursday 22 January 1948

Ella Fitzgerald and the Illinois Jacquet Group play a concert at the Academy of Music in Philadelphia.

Friday 23 January 1948
Ella Fitzgerald and the Illinois Jacquet Group play a concert at the Mosque Auditorium in Newark, New Jersey.

Saturday 24 January 1948
Ella Fitzgerald and the Illinois Jacquet Group play a matinee at the Masonic Auditorium in Rochester and an evening concert (8.30pm) at Kleinhan's Music Hall in Buffalo, New York.

Sunday 25 January 1948
Ella Fitzgerald and the Illinois Jacquet Group play a matinee at the I.M.A. Auditorium in Flint, Michigan, and an evening concert at the Masonic Temple in Detroit.

Monday 26 January 1948
Ella Fitzgerald and the Illinois Jacquet Group play a concert in Cincinnati, Ohio.

Tuesday 27 January 1948
Ella Fitzgerald and the Illinois Jacquet Group play a concert in Cleveland, Ohio.

Wednesday 28 January 1948
Ella Fitzgerald and the Illinois Jacquet Group play a concert at the Syria Mosque in Pittsburgh, Pennsylvania.

Thursday 29 January 1948
Ella Fitzgerald and the Illinois Jacquet Group play a concert in Louisville, Kentucky.

Friday 30 January 1948
Ella Fitzgerald and the Illinois Jacquet Group play a concert at the Civic Opera House in Chicago.

Saturday 31 January 1948
Ella Fitzgerald and the Illinois Jacquet Group play a concert at the Kiel Auditorium in St. Louis, Missouri.

Sunday 1 February 1948
Ella Fitzgerald and the Illinois Jacquet Group play a concert at the Masonic Auditorium in Detroit.

Monday 2 February 1948
Ella Fitzgerald and the Illinois Jacquet Group play a concert in Minneapolis.

Tuesday 10 February 1948
Ella Fitzgerald opens a one-week engagement at the Swing Club in Oakland, California.

Sunday 15 February 1948
Ella Fitzgerald closes at the Swing Club in Oakland, California.

Wednesday 18 February 1948
Ella Fitzgerald opens a four-week engagement at Billy Berg's club in Los Angeles, California.

Ella Fitzgerald's sudden exit from Billy Berg's is the talk of the town. It's being widely cocktail-roomered in the sin spots of Hollywood that she closed (a week ahead of schedule) because she and the management just couldn'e see eye to eye on certain matters of great interest to her . . .

Tuesday 9 March 1948
Ella Fitzgerald closes a week early at Billy Berg's club in Los Angeles, California.

Friday 12 March 1948

Ella and Mel Torme open a two-week engagement at the State-Lake Theatre in Chicago.

Chicago—All these pretty people (plus Henry Brandon's house band, the other three members of Monti's Tu Tones and the five members of Herbie Fields' band) are members of a fabulous stage show which appeared recently at the State-Lake theater here. Production, engineered by Nate Platt of Balaban & Katz, included four Chicago disc jockeys, singer Mel Torme, at the drums, Ella Fitzgerald, and the groups of Monti and Fields. Left to right around Torme are Ernie Simon, Ella, Linn Burton, Eddie Hubbard, Monti, Dave Garroway, and Fields. Reports are that show didn't get good audience reaction, but grossed $38,000. Staff photo by Ted.

Sunday 14 March 1948

Ella Fitzgerald broadcasts on the 'Dave Garroway Show' in Chicago.

Thursday 25 March 1948

Ella and Mel Torme close at the State-Lake Theatre in Chicago.

Monday 5 April 1948

Ella Fitzgerald opens a one-week engagement at the Copa Club in Pittsburgh.

Saturday 10 April 1948

Ella Fitzgerald closes at the Copa Club in Pittsburgh.

Tuesday 13 April 1948

Ella Fitzgerald in a Dream Show benefit concert for the Booker T Washington Memorial Fund at Carnegie Hall in New York City. Also on the bill are Duke Ellington's Orchestra minus Duke, Carmen Miranda, Zero Mostel, Robert Merrill, Gladys Swarthout and The Charioteers.

Wednesday 21 April 1948

Ella Fitzgerald opens a four-week engagement at the Paramount Theatre in New York City. Also on the bill are Duke Ellington and his Orchestra, The Four Step Brothers and George Kirby. The movie presentation is 'The Big Clock' starring Ray Milland and Charles Laughton.

New York—Somebody should enter the Ellington-Fitzgerald show at the Paramount theater in the Memorial Day race at Indianapolis. It moves faster than anything on wheels. Here is a show that combines the talents of two of the hottest attractions in the music business, attractions which easily could use the entire show time to their own individual advantage without fully satisfying the customers. The band's contributions are few but somehow manage to show off all departments to advantage. Two instrumentals give star sidemen the necessary opportunities, **How High The Moon** being the opener, and a special concert arrangement of **Frankie And Johnny** taking the halfway spot. Kay Davis does her familiar **On A Turquoise Cloud** and, aside from exceptional accompaniment for the Four Step Brothers, that about takes care of the band. Ella does three tunes, **Robbins Nest, Can't Help Lovin' That Man** and, of course, **Lady Be Good**. She is followed by a mimic, George Kirby, who does the usual run-of-the-mill imitations of movie and radio stars, then kills the audience by doing a perfect take-off of Ella doing the number she'd just finished, **Lady Be Good**. That old axiom of show business, "always leave them wanting more," is applied here for the show as a whole and for the artists individually. This kind of stuff is a hypo for both band and show biz.

Sunday 25 April 1948

Ella Fitzgerald's 30th birthday.

Thursday 29 April 1948

Ella Fitzgerald records with The Song Spinners and a studio orchestra for Decca in New York City.

ELLA FITZGERALD, THE SONG SPINNERS (vocal), studio orchestra

Tea Leaves

Friday 30 April 1948

Ella Fitzgerald records with The Song Spinners for Decca in New York City.

ELLA FITZGERALD, THE SONG SPINNERS (vocal)

My Happiness

Wednesday 5 May 1948

Down Beat reviews Ella's latest record releases:

Ella Fitzgerald
** *Darktown Strutters Ball*
** *Shine*

These must be reissues, for they feature Ella only as the vocalist in what were apparently original straight band sides. The great lady usually can do no wrong, but these sides are from her not fully developed past and are a far cry from her present work. **Ball** has Ella at the beginning and end, with baritone, piano and clarinet choruses; the latter sounding much like Buster Bailey's up and down the scale style. **Shine** has only incidental Ella also. (*Decca 25354*)

Ella Fitzgerald
**** *How High The Moon*
*** *You Turned The Tables On Me*

Come back Ella—all is forgiven. All **High** is divided into three parts of which the firstis a straight vocal, the second an up tempo phrased and differently worded chorus and the third a scatter, bop style, like her **Lady Be Good**. **Tables** gets conventional styling which from Ella is all this and heaven too. (*Decca 24387*)

Tuesday 18 May 1948

Ella Fitzgerald closes at the Paramount Theatre in New York City.

Friday 28 May 1948

Ella Fitzgerald opens a one-week engagement at the Broadway Capitol Theatre in Detroit. The Harmonicats share the bill.

Friday 3 June 1948

Ella Fitzgerald closes at the Broadway Capitol Theatre in Detroit.

Thursday 10 June 1948

Ella Fitzgerald and the Ray Brown Trio open a four-week engagement at the Three Deuces on 52nd Street in New York City.

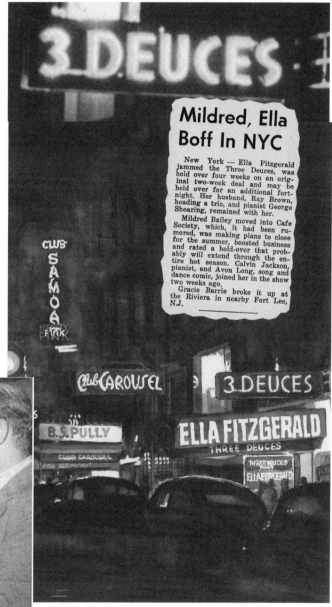

Mildred, Ella Boff In NYC

New York — Ella Fitzgerald jammed the Three Deuces, was held over four weeks on an original two-week deal and may be held over for an additional fortnight. Her husband, Ray Brown, heading a trio, and pianist George Shearing, remained with her.

Mildred Bailey moved into Cafe Society, which, it had been rumored, was making plans to close for the summer, boosted business and rated a hold-over that probably will extend through the entire hot season. Calvin Jackson, pianist, and Avon Long, song and dance comic, joined her in the show two weeks ago.

Gracie Barrie broke it up at the Riviera in nearby Fort Lee, N.J.

Left: Booker Moe Gale and Decca recording executive Milt Gabler, along with Duke Ellington and Benny Goodman, are at the Three Deuces to present Ella with a cake celebrating her tenth anniversary as "First Lady of Song."

Extend Ella's Stay At Deuces To July 7; Talk 10-Year Pact

NEW YORK CITY—Ella Fitzgerald, the first lady of song, is going over with a bang at the Three Deuces, on 52nd St., in New York, and nightclub manager Sammy Kaye knows it.

The nitery impresario offered Ella a brand new contract which extends her stay at the New York club until July 7.

The new contract also calls for Ella to make one appearance per year at the Three Deuces for the next 10 years.

Ever since her opening on June 10, Ella Fitzgerald has been the toast of New York. On opening night a host of celebrities, including Nat "King" Cole, Duke Ellington, Artie Shaw, Ethel Smith, Henry Morgan, Benny Goodman, Art Tatum and Kay Starr turned out to pay tribute to the songstress who is celebrating her 10th Anniversary as a headliner.

Ella Turns Out A Two Bagger

NEW YORK—When one side of a phonograph record becomes a contender for the hit parade class, that's a rarity. When both sides of a single disc reach that stage, that's news!

several weeks ago, Decca records released a new disc by Ella Fitzgerald. Almost immediately the juke box operators, the disc jockies, the retailers and the public acclaimed one of the sides, "My Happiness", as the hit of the near future. Billboard, the theatrical weekly publication, listed "My Happiness" at the top of its possibilities list. A week later, Variety—the theatrical newspaper—recorded the news that "My Happiness", by Ella Fitzgerald, had reached the best seller class.

Last week, Billboard noted the fact that although "My Happiness" was steadily climbing the best seller list, it was being crowded by another record. The competing disc turned out to be Ella's recording of "Tea Leaves"—the "B" side of "Happiness."

Wednesday 7 July 1948
Ella Fitzgerald closes at the Three Deuces on 52nd Street in New York City.

Saturday 17 July 1948
Ella Fitzgerald appears at the American Music Festival at White Sox Park in Chicago.

Sunday 18 July 1948
Ella Fitzgerald makes her first television appearance on Ed Sullivan's Show, 'Toast of the Town' in New York City. She sings *Mr Paganini*.

Wednesday 21 July 1948
Ella Fitzgerald and the Ray Brown Trio play afternoon and evening concerts (2.30 & 8.30pm) at the World's Fair of Music, Grand Central Palace, Lexington Avenue at 46th Street in New York City.
A-Tisket, A-Tasket / Cow Cow Boogie / Oh, Lady Be Good / Nature Boy / Summertime / The Woody Woodpecker Song

Wednesday 28 July 1948
Ella Fitzgerald broadcasts on 'Swing Time at the Savoy' in New York City.

Monday 2 August 1948
Ella Fitzgerald broadcasts on 'Patterns in Melody' in New York City.

Friday 13 August 1948
Ella Fitzgerald and the Ray Brown Trio open a one-week engagement at the Apollo Theatre in New York City. Also on the bill are Boyd Raeburn and his Orchestra.

Thursday 19 August 1948
Ella Fitzgerald and the Ray Brown Trio close at the Apollo Theatre in New York City.

Friday 20 August 1948
Ella Fitzgerald records with the Illinois Jacquet Quartet for Decca in New York City.
ELLA FITZGERALD (vocal), ILLINOIS JACQUET (tenor sax), unknown piano, bass and drums
It's Too Soon / I Can't Go On Without You

Friday 20 August 1948
Ella Fitzgerald and the Ray Brown Trio open a one-week engagement at the Howard Theatre in Washington, D.C.

Thursday 26 August 1948
Ella Fitzgerald and the Ray Brown Trio close at the Howard Theatre in Washington, D.C.

Tuesday 31 August 1948
Ella Fitzgerald and the Ray Brown Trio open a 12-day engagement at the Rag Doll in Chicago.

Chicago Raves As Ella Fitzgerald Triumphs In Bon Voyage Date Here

There is a sentimental significance in Ella Fitzgerald's decision to accept a brief engagement in Chicago prior to her departure for a London appearance at the Palladium. The name of the Chicago rendezvous where Ella opens on August 31 for a 12 day stay, is the Rag Doll. And thereby hangs a tale.

Traditional object of childhood's affection is the Rag Doll. Therefore, with the genial superstition of a trouper, Ella saw a good omen in the Rag Doll booking which was offered to her. She accepted the Chicago offering both because of the omen she saw in the club's name and because she wanted to give her many fans a last opportunity to see and hear her before she began her trip to England.

The significance of the Rag Doll to Ella Fitzgerald is not apparent until it is revealed that the famed songstress was raised in an orphanage. Throughout her years in the Orphan Asylum, Ella's only possession on which she could shower affection was a Rag Doll. She clung to the small doll like a child with parents clings to its mother's skirts.

Years later, after Ella had left the orphanage and become recognized as one of show business' truly great performers, she was approached by Mrs. Edna Blue, chairman of the then newly-organized Foster Parents Plan. Mrs. Blue told Ella that the organization was trying to supply each war-orphaned child with a foster parent who, through the Plan, would receive food, clothing and playthings every month. Ella was immediately impressed with the idea and accepted.

Above: Ella Fitzgerald on stage at the Rag Doll in Chicago, accompanied by Hank Jones (piano), Ray Brown (bass) and Charlie Smith (drums).

Saturday 11 September 1948
Ella Fitzgerald closes at the Rag Doll in Chicago.

Pat Harris, of *Down Beat*, reviews the show at the Rag Doll:

'I Don't Like To Sing Bop Most,' says Ella

Chicago—"I don't like to sing bop." It was no one less than Ella Fitzgerald saying that, and if she hadn't qualified it with a "most," it would have shattered the illusions of thousands of her fans. Ella does like to sing bop syllables. She thinks it's a lot of fun. But she likes ballads best. "I like to tell a story," Ella explained.

"Riffin' is fun, but it gets monotonous," she mused, admitting wryly that as far as the audience is concerned, she could sing *How High the Moon* all night.

Mostly Sweet

What Ella sang, when we heard her at the Rag Doll here, was mostly sweet, though the songs themselves easily could have had a jump treatment. The phrase "something sweet and gentle" from *Robbins Nest* typified her mood.

She sang *Them There Eyes, Don't Worry 'Bout Me, If You Ever Should Leave*, and, to balance these four, *My Baby Loves to Be-bop* and a calypso number about Moe and Joe. That makes the score four to two, in favor of the sweet. Clincher was the encore, when the audience clamored for *Flying Home*. She sang *Nature Boy*.

By "sweet," don't think we mean without experimentation and interpolation and the constant musicianship she exhibits when she sings. But you can't be gentle with a jump tune, and Miss Fitzgerald was feeling very gentle indeed. How long this lasts, we have no way of knowing.

Perfect Setting

One night at the Rag Doll the electric power failed in the whole block for an hour and a half. Patrons saw Ella by candlelight for one set, and it must have fitted perfectly.

Ella, who likes club work best because it leaves her some freedom to do things a little differently, also likes having persons sitting around her when she sings, rather than far out front, as in the Rag Doll.

She reports that she has been singing more of the "old songs" recently. "What can you do with *Woody Woodpecker*?" she asks.

Sunday 12 September 1948
Ella and Ray Brown have a farewell party takes place at the Three Deuces where George Shearing is playing.

Tuesday 14 September 1948
Ella Fitzgerald and Ray Brown, with pianist Hank Jones, leave for London aboard the *Queen Mary*. During the voyage Ella, Ray and Hank take part in jam sessions with members of the Ivor Noone and Paul Raye QM orchestras. Ella says: "Laurie Morgan is a grand drummer and quite a character."

Melody Maker

INCORPORATING   "RHYTHM"

SEPTEMBER 25, 1948   [Registered at the G.P.O. as a Newspaper]   THREEPENCE

Monday 20 September 1948

The *Queen Mary* docks in Southampton. Ella Fitzgerald and Ray Brown take the train to London.

Tuesday 21 September 1948

Ray Brown visits Archer Street with Jack Parnell and other members of the Ted Heath Orchestra.

Monday 27 September 1948

Ella Fitzgerald opens a one-week engagement at the Empire Theatre, Glasgow. She is suffering from a heavy cold, but sings *Cow Cow Boogie / Don't Worry 'Bout Me / Woody Woodpecker / Nature Boy / A-Tisket A-Tasket / My Happiness*

September 1948

Metronome features Ella and Ray in the Blindfold Test:

ELLA IS HERE WITH GILLESPIE BASSIST HUSBAND

ON Monday evening last (20th), as was exclusively forecast on the front page of our previous issue, famous Negro vocalist Ella Fitzgerald arrived in London following her disembarkation from the "Queen Mary" at Southampton.

With Ella is her famous bassist husband, Ray Brown, formerly a mainstay of the Dizzy Gillespie Orchestra, and Brunswick recording pianist Henry "Hank" Jones, the latter of whom will accompany the singer during her stage appearances in this country.

As previously reported, Ella will be opening next Monday (27th) at the Empire, Glasgow, and will follow her engagement there by appearing at the London Palladium as an extra added attraction at the top season opening the fortnight commencing October 4.

To all enthusiasts of modern style swing singing, Ella Fitzgerald's arrival in Britain is an event of paramount interest. Known as America's first lady of song, a first-rate singer in the accepted style who is also capable of swinging ballads with equal versatility.

GENERAL ACCLAIM

At least a score of personalities of the vocalist famous Dizzy Gillespie Band, Roy Eldridge, ...

Ella and Ray have a big smile for the "M.M." camera when they get to Town.

Below: Ella and Ray settle into their London hotel.

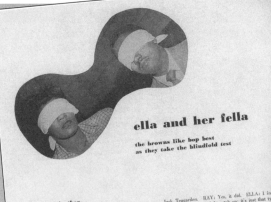

ella and her fella

the browns like bop best as they take the blindfold test

by leonard feather

TALKING MUSIC with Ella Fitzgerald is a refreshing experience. After more than a decade as one of the country's greatest popular singers (she's only 29!) Ella has retained all the enthusiasm of a newcomer, and the critical interest of a real music lover. As her wonderful performances of the past year have shown, she has kept in close touch with modern developments in jazz, having toured with the Gillespie band and cemented the relationship by marrying one of Dizzy's distinguished alumni, bassist Ray Brown.

There wasn't much disagreement between Mr. and Mrs. Brown as they shared a blindfold test. Here are their reactions to the unidentified records I played for them:

the records

1. RAY: This sounds like it was recorded around 1937-38 . . . that might be Erskine Hawkins on trumpet . . . ELLA: No, that's Roy . . . and that's Chu . . . this must be Teddy Hill's band. Either Teddy Hill or Fletcher. RAY: I never heard Teddy Hill's band . . . Isn't this something that was recorded for Benny Goodman? ELLA: For the time this was recorded, I'd give it three stars. RAY: I'd say the same, considering the age—saxophone section sounded nice; good trumpet solo. Three stars.

2. ELLA: Nice related record. I liked the guitar, and the trombone solo; I also liked the vocal. Well, I mean, at least you could understand what she was singing. RAY: I didn't care too much for the tune. Guitar was okay; vocal—just plain. Two stars, I'd say.

Jack Teagarden. RAY: Yes, it did. ELLA: I imagine it gets played a lot it might catch on; it's just that typ... her. I'd give it three stars. RAY: Now wait; we them according to how they would sell; you rate th... to how good it is. ELLA: Well, I mean, for the selling it! RAY: Okay.

3. ELLA: Sounds like that group Chubby has . . . know it's Chubby. Nice bass, nice guitar. I'll gi... stars. ELLA: I liked it, but it seemed—I don't kn... *(Continued ...)*

records reviewed by ray and ella

The Browns were given no information whatever about the records for them, either before or during the test.

1. Fletcher Henderson, *Christopher Columbus* (Vocalion)... Chu Berry, Chu, tenor; Roy Eldridge, trumpet; Jack Marsteau, guitar.
2. Julia Lee, *All I Ever Do Is Worry* (Capitol). Jack Marsteau, guitar. Benny Carter, trombone.
3. Woody Herman's Woodchoppers, *Four Men On A Horse* (Columbia). Chubby Jackson, bass; Billy Bauer, guitar.
4. Count Basie, *Ready, Set, Go* (Victor). Jeanne Taylor, vocal (not the girl Ella was thinking about).
5. Benny Goodman Sextet, *Cherokee* (Capitol). Red Norvo, vibes.
6. Coleman Hawkins, *Bean At The Met* (Keynote). Hawkins, tenor; Roy Eldridge, trumpet; Teddy Wilson, piano.
7. Billie Stewart (imitating Billie Holiday), *Solitude* (Savoy).
8. Claude Thornhill, *Anthropology* (Columbia). Lee Konitz, alto; Barry Galbraith, guitar.
9. Stan Kenton, *Lonely Woman* (Capitol). Comp. Benny Carter; lyrics by Ray Sonin; arr. by Pete Rugolo; June Christy, vocal.
10. Charlie Parker, *Relaxing At Camarillo* (Dial). Barney Kessel, guitar.

METRONOME

18

Saturday 2 October 1948

Ella Fitzgerald closes at the Empire Theatre, Glasgow.

Monday 4 October 1948

Ella Fitzgerald opens a two-week engagement at the London Palladium. Top of the bill is Gracie Fields.

Saturday 16 October 1948
Ella Fitzgerald closes at the London Palladium.

Sunday 17 October 1948
Ella Fitzgerald makes an appearance on a Sunday Night Swing Session with her trio and the Ted Heath Orchestra at the London Palladium.
It's Magic / How High The Moon / Oh, Lady Be Good / Oop Pop A Da / That's My Desire / Flying Home / Run, Joe

ELLA SLAYS 'EM WITH TED HEATH

THE EAR-SPLITTING OVATION GIVEN TO GUEST SINGER ELLA FITZGERALD AT TED HEATH'S LONDON PALLADIUM SWING SESSION LAST SUNDAY EVENING (17th) FAR SURPASSED THAT AFFORDED ANY SWING ARTIST APPEARING ON THE BRITISH STAGE SINCE THE WAR.

This overwhelming reception must have more than made up for any disappointments felt by the popular American since she arrived here to find herself singing, not her usual type of number to gatherings of fans, but an over-commercialised programme to very "family" audiences at the London Palladium.

There is no doubt that Ella thoroughly enjoyed her two sessions with the Ted Heath Orchestra, augmented for the occasion by Ella's husband, Ray Brown, who conducted the band when he was not playing bass; Hank Jones, Ella's piano accompanist; and the redoubtable Ray Ellington on drums.

The occasion marked Ella's first appearance before an out-and-out swing audience of British enthusiasts; and again and again she was recalled by the bop-hungry semi-hysterical fans who seemed determined to keep America's "First Lady of Song" on the stage until midnight. It was, indeed, only when regulations compelled him to do so that Ted Heath, with obvious reluctance, brought the memorable session to a close.

Only during Ella's first number was there a trace of the nervousness noticed by our reviewer at the Palladium opening a fortnight earlier. Warmed by the lusty applause, she quickly got into her stride, singing mostly rebop and novelty numbers with verve and immense swing.

ELLA IMPRESSED

When Ray Brown, on bass, took the Heath band through his famous arrangement of "One Bass Hit," Ella danced and jived in front of the orchestra and was clearly immensely impressed by the performance—in particular by Kenny Baker's stratospheric trumpet passages.

Ella sang sometimes with the orchestra, sometimes with a trio comprising Hank Jones, Ray Brown and Ray Ellington. Her numbers included "It's Magic," "How High The Moon," "Lady Be Good," "Oo-Pop-A-Da," "That's My Desire," "Flying Home" and "Run, Joe," the last-named a calypso which she put over with considerable energy.

Before Ella made her appearance the packed house had been well entertained by the Ted Heath band (playing in great form), the swing contingents respectively led by Kenny Baker and Jack Parnell, and the Ray Ellington Quartet. Unquestionably, this was the most outstandingly successful concert of an always popular series.

This week, Ella is appearing at the Empire, Newcastle, and after returning to London during the week-end she will take a rest until her departure for the States on the "Queen Elizabeth" on Saturday (30th). Offers have been received for her to play concerts here and in France, but the MELODY MAKER understands that she is not expected to make any more public appearances this trip.

The ear-splitting ovation given to guest singer Ella Fitzgerald at Ted Heath's London Palladium Swing Session last Sunday evening far surpassed that afforded any swing artist appearing on the British stage s[...]

Melody Maker, England's top mus[...]

ELLA FITZGERALD LEAVES

"Melody Maker" scribe, Max Jones and cameraman Jack Marshall were at Waterloo Station last Saturday (30th) to bid the stars adieu when pre-eminent U.S. songstress Ella Fitzgerald, husband Ray Brown, and pianist Hank Jones caught the boat train for the "Queen Elizabeth," en route for home, after their eventful visit to England.

Our picture shows (l. to r.): Ray Brown, Ella Fitzgerald, Ted Heath bassist Charlie Short and Hank Jones.

Monday 18 October 1948
Ella Fitzgerald opens a one-week engagement at the Empire Theatre in Newcastle.

Saturday 23 October 1948
Ella Fitzgerald closes at the Empire Theatre in Newcastle.

Saturday 30 October 1948
Ella Fitzgerald and Ray Brown catch the boat train from Waterloo to Southampton for the trip home aboard the *Queen Elizabeth*.

November 1948

Metronome reviews Ella's latest Decca release:

Ella Fitzgerald

It's Too Soon To Know C+
I Can't Go On B–

This date must have been made just before the ban, otherwise Ella would not have recorded with such a cold. Unfortunately for her, there is a very tired, unnamed male quartet harassing her every move on *Soon*. A miserable, out-of-tune tenor leads into a horrible background for the great lady on the second tune, which she sings more fluidly. (Decca 24497)

Wednesday 10 November 1948

Ella Fitzgerald records for Decca in New York City.
ELLA FITZGERALD (vocal), unknown accompaniment
To Make A Mistake Is Human / In My Dreams

Friday 12 November 1948

Ella Fitzgerald and the Ray Brown Trio open a one-week engagement at the Paradise Theatre in Detroit. The Erskine Hawkins Orchestra are also on the bill.

Detroit Welcomes Ella After Her Trip Abroad

DETROIT—In case Detroit's census takers are wondering what ever happened to more than two thousand citizens the other afternoon, they can breathe easily. The missing citizens would have been found packed into the Paradise Theatre listening to Ella Fitzgerald sing and Erskine Hawkins' Orchestra play.

Early in the morning, on opening day, a line began to form outside of the Paradise Theatre's box office and kept growing until the theatre opened. The first show of the day played to standing room only and the crowds didn't decrease the rest of the day.

The reason for this sudden rise in business, explained the Paradise manager, was that Ella Fitzgerald had just returned from London and this date was her first theatre engagement since her return. Another reason for the crowds was the Erskine Hawkins orchestra which has gained many fans since the Hawk came up with his recent innovation, the Erskine Hawkins Dance Carnival.

Thursday 18 November 1948

Ella Fitzgerald and the Ray Brown Trio close at the Paradise Theatre in Detroit.

Tuesday 23 November 1948

Ella Fitzgerald and the Ray Brown Trio open a two-week engagement at the Royal Roost in New York City. Sharing the bill are Lester Young's Sextet (Lester, tenor sax; Jesse Drakes, trumpet; Ted Kelly, trombone; Freddy Jefferson, piano; Tex Briscoe, bass; Roy Haynes, drums) and Tadd Dameron.

Ella Fitzgerald 'Takes' Broadway

NEW YORK—Bowing into the Royal Roost with such top supporting musical talent as the Ray Brown Trio and Lester Young's Combo, Ella Fitzgerald made New York stand up and cheer last Tuesday night.

Capacity business for the Ella Fitzgerald opening was predicted by manager Watkins when he hung her picture on his Wall of Fame even before her opening. The Roost's Wall of Fame is reserved only for those performers who play to continuous Standing Room Only audiences at the club. But the Roost's manager had received so many advance reservations that he decided to stick his neck out and put the picture up in advance.

For Ella, it was the first appearance in a nightclub since her recent return from London.

Twelve years ago Ella predicted the current Be-Bop trend by recording a tune called "Tain't What Cha Do" in which she closed with the words "Re-Bop."

Saturday 27 November 1948

Ella Fitzgerald broadcasts from the Royal Roost in New York City.
ELLA FITZGERALD (vocal), HANK JONES (piano), RAY BROWN (bass), CHARLIE SMITH (drums)
Oh, Lady Be Good / I Never Knew / Love That Boy (vEF) / *Too Soon To Know* (vEF) / *Mr. Paganini* (vEF) / *Royal Roost Bop Boogie* (vEF)

Saturday 4 December 1948

Ella Fitzgerald broadcasts from the Royal Roost in New York City.
ELLA FITZGERALD (vocal), HANK JONES (piano), RAY BROWN (bass), CHARLIE SMITH (drums)
Tiny's Blues / Bop Goes The Weasel / Heat Wave (vEF) / *Old Mother Hubbard* (vEF) / *Royal Roost Bop Boogie* (vEF) / *Flying Home* (vEF)

Wednesday 8 December 1948

Ella Fitzgerald and the Ray Brown Trio close at the Royal Roost in New York City.

Thursday 16 December 1948

Ella Fitzgerald and the Ray Brown Trio play a concert at the Civic Auditorium in Toledo, Ohio.

Friday 24 December 1948

Ella Fitzgerald and the Ray Brown Trio open a two-week engagement at the Club Astoria in Baltimore, Maryland.

Ella Plays Show For Chick Webb Shrine

More than ten years ago the late Chick Webb heard a young singer at the old Harlem Opera House and helped start her on the road to success. Before he died, the bandleader saw his protege become one of the most popular songstresses in the country. Ella Fitzgerald, who was the young singer, never forgot all that Chick Webb did for her and every year she has paid tribute to him in some way.

This year Ella made an appearance at the Chick Webb Memorial Center, which is run for the benefit of the underprivileged children of Baltimore, to entertain the youngsters at a Yule party.

To make certain that an unexpected engagement would not keep her from making the appearance at the center, Ella had her office book her into the Club Astoria, in Baltimore, for the ten days which embrace the holiday season.

She has never forgotten that it was Chick Webb who gave her the first break she ever had and it is fitting that she was chosen to be the performer to entertain at the Chick Webb Memorial Center this year.

INDEX

INDEX